Donald G. Richter

Here Stands The Law

United Graphic, Inc.
Mattoon, IL

For information, address the Vermilion County Museum Society, 116 N. Gilbert Street, Danville, IL 61832-8506

Library of Congress Catalogue Number 2001 130968

ISBN 0-9654976-4-X

First Edition

This book is dedicated to

Sheriff Hardy Whitlock
State's Attorney John Keeslar
Judge Morton Thompson

They believed in the law.

All proceeds from the sale of this book
will benefit the
Vermilion County Museum Society

Acknowledgments

Many people assisted in obtaining the information contained in this book. It would not have been completed in this form without the help of Margaret Gunn Hickman, Ruth Thompson McGibeny, Katherine Stapp, Jake Baker, Camilla Hegeler Buckingham, and Tracy Warbritton.

Hickman is the daughter of former Illinois Supreme Court Justice Walter T. Gunn. He studied law under John Keeslar, the state's attorney who is a prominent figure in this book. Gunn was also an assistant state's attorney under Keeslar and became his law partner. Many of the historical facts, relating to Sheriff Whitlock, were documented through the Keeslar/Gunn relationship.

Ruth Thompson McGibeny is the niece of Judge Morton B. Thompson. The Judge presided over the trial which is documented in this work. The events recorded in this volume were recounted a number of times by Thompson to his niece. Though he handled many cases during his long career, McGibeny recalled it was this case that he was most proud of. I am indebted to her for loaning correspondence relating to the case and for her many patient answers to my numerous inquiries. Historian Katherine Stapp was intrigued by this event which shook Danville. It was from her that I obtained notes on the comments of A.B. Dennis as well as other information relating to the riot and its aftermath.

Jacob Baker worked in the coal mines with Isaac Slade and Horace Murphy. He passed on information obtained from these two participants in the riot. Camilla Hegeler Buckingham supplied information pertaining to the George T. Buckingham/Sheriff Whitlock relationship. Attorney George T. Buckingham had an illustrious career that included serving as President of the Board of Joliet

State Penitentiary and as a Trustee of Kankakee State Hospital. He is mentioned prominently in this book and his remembrances, passed on by Camilla Buckingham, were very helpful. The George T. Buckingham diary and personal correspondence aided immeasurably in recording the events as they happened.

Tracy Warbritton was unrelenting in her search of the court records to supply as many facts as possible for this project. I am deeply indebted to her for the numerous court documents she unearthed in her search of legal papers. Others who contributed were, Ireta Bremer, Attorney Francis "Frank" Brittingham, Richard Cannon, Ruth Burcham Howard, Webber Graves, Attorney Horace Gunn, Clarence Plymire, Otis Ranger, Edgar Richter, Jesse Trent, and Frances Watkins.

The staff of the Illinois State Historical Library and Doctor Wayne Temple of the Illinois State Archives were also of great assistance.

I am grateful to my wife Susan, who typed and put into book form the rough draft I had assembled. I would also like to thank Kathy Darding for all the time she spent proof reading the manuscript.

As a matter of information for researchers, the following newspaper sources were used extensively; *Danville Commercial News*, July-October 1903; *Danville Press*, July-October 1903; *Chicago Tribune*, July-August 1903; *Chicago Chronicle*, July-August 1903; *Danville Democrat*, July-October 1903.

Prologue

Sheriff Hardy Whitlock stood resolutely on the porch of the Vermilion County jail. The brick and stone building crouched like a small fortress on the west side of South Vermilion Street in Danville. In his large hands he held a Winchester shotgun. In front of the jail, brick paved Vermilion Street was filled with a mob of shouting, threatening people. These people he knew. They were the public he exchanged greetings with each day on the street. They were the voters who had put him in office.

Now they seemed possessed by an insane rage, determined to continue the rampage of violence which had already resulted in the murder of one man. As the Sheriff felt the cold metal of the weapon in his hands and contemplated his next move, he had to wonder if there was anyone in the city who was not on the streets. The crowd was backed up for blocks from the brick jail building. It was a mob of opposites; ministers and saloon keepers, elderly men and young boys, attorneys and men with criminal records, laboring men and business leaders, house wives and prostitutes. There were people in the mob who had walked the streets of Danville with Abraham Lincoln when he had a law office in the city. They had heard the cannon roar in the great War Between the States. Now they all seemed united in a common purpose.

The hot, night air was filled with smoke from a small, smoldering fire at the corner of South and Vermilion Streets. If one looked closely at the burning straw and railroad ties, the mutilated body of a man could be seen at the center of the fire.

The street lights had all been broken out and the only illumination of the tense scene came from the bright lights on the jail's porch, and from the lanterns and torches carried by members of the mob.

The Sheriff wiped the sweat from his face and shouted for one of his deputies to come to the porch. Deputy David Newlin came out the front door of the jail. The Sheriff handed him the riot gun he had been holding and instructed the young man to take it back inside.

The lawman then left the brightly lit porch and entered the twilight area of the mob. No sheriff in the United States had ever defended his jail from a mob like this but the lawman was going to try. He knew all of the people gathered on the street were not involved in the violence, some of them were there out of curiosity. Perhaps he could bring sanity back to the city. It was July 25th, 1903.

Part 1

The Lynching and the Riot

Chapter One

Jim Wilson was a seasoned traveler of the poor man's highway. His long legs made good time as his feet made a rhythmic sound on the cinders and ballast of the Illinois Central railway bed. It was July 24, 1903 and the tall, young, black man was on his way back to his native Virginia from Bloomington, Illinois. Wilson was the son of former slaves but both of his parents were now deceased. After his father's death, he continued to live with his stepmother in the Midwest town of Bloomington. The family had left the South a number of years earlier to come north where they had been told work was more plentiful. Wilson had just learned that his step-mother was planning to return to the South and he was going ahead of her to try to find employment.

Wilson had recently been employed as a roustabout for a small circus that was touring in Pennsylvania. The show, known as the John Robinson Circus, was similar to many small traveling attractions touring the nation in the early part of the 20th century. The circus employed a number of regulars and supplemented these with part time roustabouts. When hard times overtook one of these small ventures, as they often did, the part time employees were the first to feel the effect. This had happened to Wilson in Tyron, Pennsylvania.

Robinson had announced to his employees there was no money to pay them for their time, and Wilson had been one of those on the list who was not to be paid. He and a number of the other workers had demanded payment and Robinson had at once summoned the law. The disgruntled workers had all been locked up in the local jail until the circus left town; then they had been released and Wilson had headed north. When he reached his step-mother's home in Bloomington, she had announced she was packing to return to Virginia. Wilson then decided to return to the South and try to find employment.

Now, as the man made his way along the rails, he was consumed by hunger. He had not eaten well for sometime and he was on the watch for a meal. As he would put it later, no matter what the cost. Wilson carried an old revolver with him, which rested heavily in his pocket. The gun was broken but its presence gave him a measure of security, for someone on the wrong end of the barrel would not know the weapon was useless.

It was well past noon as Wilson was making his way through Vermilion County, Illinois. The sun beat down on him without mercy as he kept up a steady pace on the rail line which stretched on endlessly between the fertile fields of corn and hay crops. An occasional sycamore or cottonwood tree sent a cooling shadow across the right of way the man was following.

It was late afternoon when the weary traveler neared the city limits of the small village of Alvin, Illinois. Like many other towns of the period, Alvin sprung up around the railroad and now it was a thriving village. It boasted two grain elevators, two hotels, a number of grocery and dry goods stores, and a billiard parlor and saloon. The residents were even contemplating the novel idea of concrete sidewalks to front the dirt streets that ran through the village. Alvin was also the home of Tom Burgess. His house was located near the railroad tracks that ran through the village. Burgess was a section worker on the railroad and on this day he was out on the line.

Wilson walked slowly toward the village of Alvin. He noticed the small town seemed nearly deserted. He left the Illinois Central line at the junction with the C&EI tracks and made his way into the village. The Burgess home was located near the tracks and as the traveler neared the dwelling, he caught the unmistakable scent of food cooking. Wilson left the rails and slowly made his way to the tiny cottage.

Mary Burgess and her baby had spent the morning in Marshfield, Indiana and had returned to Alvin on the 1:00 P.M. train. She had been raised in the small Hoosier village and had been visiting relatives. The woman had spent the afternoon working in the family vegetable garden. When her infant became sleepy, she took the baby in and laid her on a pallet in the bedroom to sleep. The mother then went to a building behind the house to obtain a bucket of corn cobs to be used as fuel in her cooking stove.

Jim Wilson slipped quietly to the front of the Burgess house and walked onto the small porch. When he reached the screen door, he looked into the parlor and could neither hear nor see anyone. He silently opened the unlocked door and entered the home. He had only walked a few steps when he found himself at the door that led to the dining room. On a table in that room was part of the evening meal. To Wilson the table seemed to be laden with food. The intruder carefully closed the open doors and windows of the house. He still did not see anyone. He had just completed this task when from the bedroom the infant let out a lusty cry.

Burgess heard Corinne crying and left the shed to return to the house and check on the infant. She was surprised to find the door closed but thought perhaps the wind had slammed it shut. She entered the house through the covered back porch and walked through the dining room to the parlor. Before she had time to observe the closed front door and the windows that had been shut, strong hands grasped her throat and began to strangle her. As the young woman attempted to fight back, she was thrown to the floor. She struggled to free herself from the hold that was choking the life out of her. For a moment the pressure on her throat was released and she gave a piercing scream. The scream of Burgess and the crying of the baby reached the ears of the Maines family who lived next door. Hannah Maines called out to her daughter and then ran to the Burgess home.

Wilson and his victim both heard the voice from the Maines' home. Wilson would claim later he had assaulted the woman because he was afraid. He now shoved the woman away from him and raced toward the back door. He knew there was a good chance he would be decorating the end of a rope if he were caught after attacking the woman.

Hannah Maines and her daughter found Burgess at her front door screaming, "My, baby! "Oh, my baby!" Maines at once thought the baby had been injured in some manner but then the hysterical Burgess pointed to the back door and said, "That man." Maines then ran out the back door but all she could see was Wilson running away. It was clear to her the man was not kidnapping the child.

Wilson was bounding off the covered back porch of the Burgess home before the door swung shut behind him. He could hear the screams of Burgess and the calls of her neighbors as he ran. He sprinted down an alley toward the railroad tracks and heard a door slam. Looking over his shoulder Wilson could see a woman staring after him. The sight of the Maines woman watching him made him run even faster. He knew he had to hide if he were to remain free, perhaps if he were to remain alive.

The neighbor then returned and reassured the terror stricken young woman that her child was not being taken. She then went for a doctor and had word sent to the Vermilion County sheriff that a woman in Alvin had been attacked by a black man. She described him as being young and large.

Doctor George W. Howard lived nearby in the south end of Alvin. He came and examined the victim of the assault and found that she had no serious injuries. He treated the lacerations about her mouth and told her they would soon heal. The marks caused by Wilson's fingers on the face and throat of Burgess would be visible for several days before going away. The doctor also examined the infant but could find no marks or bruises on the baby. Hannah Maines remained with the terrified assault victim until her husband could be notified to return home. He was working with a railroad section crew about three miles from the village when the incident took place.

Wilson reached the tracks and his pounding feet carried him out of the small village at a dead run. He knew that Danville was the largest town in the area and he thought if he could reach it he might be able to hide there. His breathing soon became labored and he slowed his pace from a run to a steady trot as he put more distance between himself and the small village where he had just committed a crime. The sun was sinking lower in the west and in a few hours darkness would cover him and bring relief from the searing heat that was sapping his strength. For the moment, all thoughts of hunger were forgotten as survival became uppermost in the man's mind.

Word soon spread through Alvin about the attack on the Burgess woman, and men started organizing to search for the assailant. The first out were three men on a section car. They had heard of the assault while they were working at the edge of town repairing a switch. The three men immediately put their car on the track and began pumping the handles that powered the vehicle, in a few moments they were speeding down the shiny rails. In the distance there was what appeared to be the figure of a man running between the rails. The heat shimmered near the ground and made the figure seem to appear and disappear as the small car picked up more speed.

Wilson slowed to a walk, his strength was gone. He was now putting one foot in front of the other in a tired fashion, his eyes fastened on the ground. His worn out shoes were filled with cinders and gravel but he wasn't going to stop to empty them. He didn't hear the section car speeding toward him.

The men on the car could now see Wilson clearly. He was plodding along, seemingly oblivious to their approach. The pursuers did not have firearms but they did have several tools and an ax on the car. They were now near enough for the man to hear them clearly and they shouted for him to stop.

Wilson heard someone call and he spun around on his tired legs. To his surprise there was a handcar with men on it almost upon him. Now the men were shouting for him to stop and they were waving their arms. Wilson reached into his pocket and pulled out his old revolver and pointed it at the approaching section men.

The men on the car were only a short distance from the fugitive when they saw his hand go to his pocket. They were surprised and frightened when they were confronted with a revolver. They stopped the car, and the assailant and his pursuers stared at each other for a long second. Wilson then bounded down the side of the raised rail bed and leaped over a fence into a field of tall corn. The men watched him disappear into the field and then slowly began to pump their car back in the direction from which they had come. They had not expected the man to be armed, now they were cursing because they had not brought guns.

The blades of corn sliced at the fugitive's skin as he ran blindly through the field. His tiredness was forgotten as terror pumped adrenaline into his system. He finally collapsed, exhausted, after putting several fields of corn and hay crops behind him. He had been fleeing in the opposite direction of the setting sun, which now rested like a large, red ball on the western horizon. Wilson did not know where he was, he had lost the rail lines that he usually traveled.

As he rested, he listened for the sound of a train whistle and watched for the telltale ribbon of smoke on the horizon that would mark the passage of a steam engine. In the gathering dusk he did not find either sign that would lead him back to the rails. He knew that to his east were the heavy woodlands and forested river bottoms of Indiana. He thought he might already be in the Hoosier state. There would be places where a man could hide in the bottoms. Years earlier, work and escape might have been found by chopping wood for one of the numerous steamboats that plied the waters of the Wabash. That was all history now, the railroads had replaced the river boats, no more did the deep sound of the boat whistles echo in the river valleys. Only an occasional excursion boat now steamed its way up and down the river and it would certainly not provide a fugitive black man with a means of escape.

After a brief rest Wilson regained his feet and began to walk in what he assumed to be an easterly direction, the darkness of the eastern horizon was his beacon. Behind him the sky was painted with the remains of a beautiful Midwest sunset but Wilson's eyes were fixed on the darkening sky before him and escape.

When the section crew returned to Alvin, they found a large number of people gathered about the depot. The men explained at once what had happened and they decided to obtain guns and go in search of the man who had invaded the Burgess home. Word had already gone out to the nearby communities and a similar search party was being organized in State Line, Indiana, a small village to the south and east of Alvin. Word had been sent to the county sheriff's office and had been passed on by Sheriff Whitlock to the authorities in nearby Indiana. Deputies would join the search party at first light, but it was already speculated that the fugitive might have caught a ride on one of the numerous trains which passed through the area. Word was given to the railroad security men to check all the trains passing through as well as the empty rail cars in their yards.

As the facts of the home invasion and assault were told and retold, they obtained a new dimension. Some of the search parties now thought they were seeking a rapist. For the first time there were ominous comments about having a rope handy when they caught the man.

The dirt roads were filled with plumes of dust hanging in the still, humid air as men on horseback searched the roads in the area where Wilson was last seen. Others walked through the fields and wood lots, their guns at the ready, seeking the Burgess attacker. They continued their search as the twilight faded into the blackness of a humid July night.

When it became too dark to see, the searchers returned to their homes to wait for the dawn. At first light hundreds of men would be seeking the fugitive in a large area.

Wilson walked for what seemed like hours but he was not sure he was going in the right direction. Once he had seen a group of horsemen ride by and he assumed they were searching for him, but they had not seen him in the gloom of the evening. He was tired and hungry. His skin was scratched and bleeding from making his way through brambles and other obstacles in the darkness. He decided to lay down by a grain shock and wait until the morning to proceed.

July 25th dawned with the same promise of scorching heat that had seared Illinois and Indiana on the previous day. Lazy curls of smoke drifted from the chimneys of homes in the villages and farms as wives prepared the breakfast meals on their cook stoves. The aromatic scent of frying bacon and ham spilled out into the morning air and tantalized the appetites of those near the homes.

Before the smoke from the stoves and the scent of the food had died away, men were gathering for the day's work. They were organized now and they carried their well oiled rifles, shotguns, and revolvers with them. They came from the villages of Alvin, Bismarck, and State Line. Residents from the farms that dotted the area were also ready to join the band of hunters. A search party was also formed in nearby Marshfield, Indiana. Deputies and those who were self appointed lawmen gave out terse instructions as the other men listened intently. Those with horses held the reins of their animals as the mounts stomped about, anxious to be off in the freshness of the day. Men who did not have horses were loaded into box wagons. Teams would pull them to their search areas. Word was passed that the Sheriff of Vermilion County, Illinois had warned the leaders of the posse that the man was not to be lynched if he were found. Members of the search parties were also alerted to the fact that the fugitive was armed and had pulled his gun on men the previous day.

The sun was creeping up in the eastern horizon when the bands of men began to fan out across the countryside in search of a tall, young, black man.

Wilson woke up with the sun in his eyes. He looked around him and then remembered where he was and what had happened. He stood and began to walk toward the early morning sun. He was passing through an area of small farms. Pastures and wood lots were interspersed with fields of corn and hay. Shocks of oats rested in many of the fields awaiting the threshing crews. The fugitive was careful to stay away from the houses and out of sight of the dirt roads which connected the homesteads.

As the morning passed, he began to have more confidence he would be able to escape. It was about mid-morning when he found himself in a small apple orchard bordered by a rippling stream. Wilson drank heartily from the cool water and then filled his stomach with the green apples. The exhaustion from the previous day overtook him and he decided to stretch out in the shade of one of the fruit trees and rest for a few minutes.

The search party from Marshfield had left shortly after sun up to look for the fugitive wanted in Illinois. Over a hundred men were out searching the barns, fields, and woodlands of the area. They were mainly in groups of twos and threes with larger numbers searching the fields of standing corn. The Marshfield depot was their search headquarters and they were to reassemble there at noon and compare notes.

James McHaney and Ed Wurtsbaugh were members of the Marshfield posse. They had been searching all morning and they were beginning to have doubts as to whether the object of their hunt was still in the area. The sun was almost directly overhead when the two men began to systematically search a small apple orchard. They had only gone a short distance into the orchard when they saw a man stretched out on the ground asleep. They covered the prone figure with their guns and quietly walked up to him. The man did not move as the two approached to within a few feet.

Wilson had only been laying down a few minutes when he had fallen into a deep sleep. Now he felt something digging into his ribs. When he opened his eyes, he was staring at two guns pointed at him. The fugitive regarded Wurtsbaugh and McHaney for a few seconds and then slowly got to his feet, the race was over. The two men carefully searched him and took his broken revolver. They then ordered Wilson to walk ahead of them and the three made their way out of the shade of the apple trees to a dirt road that led to Marshfield.

It was a long walk to the village and it was noon when they reached Marshfield. From the edge of the small cluster of homes that made up the town, Wilson could see a large crowd gathered around the railroad depot. As he was marched to the depot, the men who were his captors did not say a word.

When Wurtsbaugh and McHaney reached the depot, they told the crowd that was gathered to let them through. The men grouped there were mainly members of the search party that had been out all morning. When people in the village observed the two marching the black man by on the street, they came along to see what would happen next. Wilson was placed under guard in the freight section of the depot and he heard one of his captors tell the railroad agent to notify the Vermilion County Sheriff. On the outside of the building he could hear the low voices of the crowd as they talked about the capture. As he sat on the hard bench in the depot under the watchful eyes of his guards, some of his earlier terror left him. So far no one had mentioned getting a rope.

Chapter Two

Danville, Illinois sprawled along the north bank of the Vermilion River and the east bank of the North Fork. Small tentacles of the growing city crossed the rivers to the west and south. The town that had once sent military aid to the infant village of Chicago was enjoying boom times. The population had exploded from only thirteen thousand in 1890 to more than 25,000 by the turn of the century, and in the year of 1903 there was unbounded optimism for the future of the Midwestern city.

Railroads crossed the town from all four points of the compass and the rails were well polished from the heavy traffic that steamed through the city. The hours of the days and nights were punctuated by the shrill whistles of the steam engines as they blew a warning at the crossings in the city. From the train yards located in the east and northeast part of Danville the sounds of freight and passenger cars being coupled and uncoupled as they switched could be heard at any time of the day or night.

Danville was the Vermilion County seat and the land that made up the county contained some of the richest coal reserves to be found anywhere in the nation. The coal industry was a major source of employment, and thousands of Europeans had immigrated to the area to work the mines. These hard working miners realized little income from their labors but they did create prosperity for mine owners and provided freight and fuel for the railroads.

Vermilion County was also a rich agricultural area and farms dotted the landscape that had once been covered with tall prairie grass. Well traveled dirt roads crisscrossed the farm country and connected the farmsteads with the county seat. On Saturday families made their way to Danville to trade their goods and do their weekly shopping. On this particular July 25th there would be a larger number of rural people than usual in the city because there was to be a free Indian Show at the public square in the evening.

Two streets in the county seat carried most of the traffic in and out of the city. Main Street ran from east to west and travelers going east would be able to continue on the road that would lead them to Indianapolis, Indiana. West Main changed into the Old State Road that ran a crooked line to the state capitol of Springfield. It was on this road that Lincoln often made his way into the city when he was an attorney riding the Eighth Judicial Circuit. Vermilion Street ran from the river by the same name to the north edge of the city. If one continued on, the road would lead to Chicago.

The county jail building was located at 38 South Vermilion Street on the west side of the brick paved street. A block north the county courthouse stood on the northeast side of the city square. Things were quiet around these two buildings as the streets of Danville began to fill with Saturday shoppers and traders. Across the street from the jail the livery stable of John T. Leonard was busy as people brought their horses and rigs in to be stabled until later in the day. The clatter of a rare motor car could be heard at times in the city but the horseless carriages were still as rare on the streets of Danville as the sight of a short-haired woman.

A short distance west of the city a construction gang employed by Danville Street Railway and Light Company was working on a rail grade. In 1903 the five day work week had not yet been invented and the sweating men, swinging their picks, were looking forward to quitting time later in the day. Not only was it the last work day of the week but it was also payday and the laborers would be putting some hard coin in their pockets when quitting time came.

One of the workers was John Metcalf. Metcalf was proud of his ability to turn in a hard day's work. He was about thirty years old and stood over six feet tall, his 200 pound muscular build made him a valuable man in the construction trade. Builder Palmer himself had recommended Metcalf for the job, pointing out that he would give a full day's work for his pay.

Metcalf lived in Danville on Hays Street and had made his home in the city for less than a year. The area where he resided was near what was known as the "bottoms," an area of town where most of the black population resided. Metcalf would be drawing $10 in pay later in the day for his hard labor. He had no way of knowing his life was rapidly approaching its end.

The most prominent resident of Vermilion County was in New York City on this Saturday that was slowly ticking down towards an explosion in Danville. Joseph Gurney Cannon was being interviewed by a reporter in his room at the elegant Hotel Manhattan. The veteran member of the U.S. House of Representatives would be the next Speaker of that body and the newspaperman was questioning the thin, bearded Cannon about his plans for the future. The congressman, or "Uncle Joe," as he was known to his constituents back home, had just completed a meeting with President Roosevelt and other leaders at Oyster Bay. Now, as the wiry Cannon observed the reporter through a cloud of smoke from one of his trademark cigars, he seemed reluctant to talk about the meeting. Instead he informed the journalist that he was "just foolin around" during the summer recess. Instead of talking politics Cannon was in a reflective mood as he relaxed in the plush hotel chair in his suite. Uncle Joe ran his hand through his once red beard, now turned nearly white, and told the newsman stories of his native Danville. While the congressman was talking to the reporter, John Metcalf was working out the last day of his life for one of the companies in which Cannon had an interest.

On East Main Street in Danville, Charles Shermayer readied his establishment for the busy night he expected. He was the proprietor of Shermayer's Saloon and Saturday was the big day of the week for the German's business. Though competition was plentiful, there seemed to be more than enough customers for the seventy plus saloons that clustered on the streets of downtown Danville. Many residents, especially the women, viewed the drinking that took place in the county seat as a disgrace. A sheriff's deputy reported that a large part of the lawlessness that occurred in the city could be laid at the feet of the saloon keepers. In a few hours, Shermayer would be a witness to the beginning of what would be one of the darkest moments in the history of the city on the Vermilion. Now, as he waited on the few early customers and polished glasses behind the bar, all was peaceful in the city.

Kuemmerle's meat market stood at 427 East Main Street, just a few doors from Shermayer's which was at 419. It was a busy day in the market, as Saturdays always were. Delivery men were making home deliveries and in the back of the store, working on the sawdust covered floor, was a young butcher named Henry Carl Gatterman. He had been working at the market for nearly a year. Prior to his job as a meat cutter, Henry had spent four years in the U.S. Army. Gatterman was a dark-haired young man of twenty-four, he was of medium height and had a muscular build. He was well liked by the people he worked with and had many friends in the community. Though he was born in the United States and had served a tour of duty in the army, he was still referred to by those who knew him as a "German." This was because his family had immigrated to the United States from Germany and also because the young butcher lived and worked in an area made up mainly of people of German descent. Gatterman had a cheerful disposition and, like the rest of the workers on this hot and humid Saturday, was looking forward to quitting time. The girl he was to marry in the autumn, Hazel Smith, was out of town. As Smith waited in Chicago for transportation to take her to Iowa to visit relatives, Gatterman's life was rapidly nearing its conclusion.

A man who would be a principal player in the drama that would engulf Danville before the day was finished, was working on a fence on a farm northwest of the city. Winfield Baker was a tall, slender Kentuckian who had moved to Illinois from the Blue Grass State seeking work. He had found it on the George Bailey farm located about three miles from Danville. The twenty-six year old Baker was reportedly a good worker and did not cause any problems in the community where he lived. An acquaintance would note later that the Kentuckian did have a dark side that came out when he drank liquor or became angry. A reporter would describe Baker as being handsome, in a dark sort of way, with thick brown hair and a drooping mustache and pleasant features. As the farm hand went about his work of mending fences for farmer Bailey he had no way of knowing that he was a piece in a puzzle that was slowly coming together to explode in the county seat.

It was late in the forenoon on July 25th, when Bessie Dodge left her residence at the northwest corner of North and Gobin Streets in Danville. Dodge would later describe her occupation as one that "forfeited all respect usually due women." The red-haired woman came to Danville from Urbana, Illinois in 1902 after her husband had been sentenced to prison. Though Dodge reported her age as twenty-one, she looked to be in her thirties. She was a tall woman and she held her head high as she made her way out of the area known for prostitution and gambling. Dodge was attractive and once might have been described as being beautiful before age and her life style cast a hardness on her features.

As she strolled about town, her long skirt touching the sidewalk, two things made her ideal for the role she would have in the coming madness; her boldness and her hatred of blacks.

As the pendulum on the clock in the Sheriff's office in the county jail slowly ticked toward noon, a small crowd gathered in front of the building. People were asking if there was any word from the search parties that were trying to arrest the man who had assaulted the Alvin woman. Deputy Charles Runyan had been informing men all morning there was as yet no word from the posse that were combing the area for the fugitive.

Now he noted men were beginning to stay at the front of the jail. The few chairs the Sheriff kept on the long porch had quickly been filled. Others were seated on the long banister that ran along the edge of the wide verandah. As still more citizens approached and began to fill the steps that led off the porch, the deputy informed them there was no need to stay at the jail. The men, who appeared to be more curious than threatening, moved off the steps and most of the others followed.

By noon, Danville was filled with an unusually large number of people, even for a Saturday. The free Indian Show to be staged at the square in the evening and a sale at the popular Ike Stern Store had both contributed to drawing people into town. As women looked at the 25 cent children's wash dresses and shirtwaist suits and skirts for $2.48, the men went in search of more manly pursuits. Some of them went to their favorite barber shops where they could receive a haircut and shave for 20 cents. Others went to one of the many saloons where a shot of whiskey could be obtained for a few cents.

Bells on the electric streetcars of the Danville Street Railway and Light Company clanged as the cars warned horses and buggies out of their way. Among the people they were bringing to the downtown area were a number of residents from the Soldiers' Home located at the east edge of the city. Before midnight many of these veterans of the Civil War, now called moss backs and graybeards by their younger comrades, would once again hear the sound of gunfire. This time it would be in the center of their hometown.

Chapter Three

It was noon when the call came into the Vermilion County jail from Marshfield, Indiana. Sheriff Hardy Whitlock took the call and learned that a suspect had been taken into custody by the Marshfield posse. He then summoned deputies Runyan and Newlin into his office. The lawman knew feelings were running high against the man accused of assaulting the Alvin woman. He also was aware there were some reports circulating that the woman had been raped by the intruder. There had been lynchings recently in Belleville, Illinois and Evansville, Indiana. Whitlock did not think the citizens of Vermilion County would take the law into their own hands but he did not want to take any unnecessary risks. He sent Runyan to the livery to pick up a horse and rig, and he instructed Newlin to keep the front of the jail clear and to notify other deputies they might be needed before the day was over. As Saturday night was usually a busy time for all the lawmen, both city and county, Whitlock wanted his men to be on hand.

The thirty-six year old Whitlock was a broad-shouldered man who stood six feet tall. His drooping mustache gave his strong facial features a rather forbidding look. His parents, James and Eliza Henderson Whitlock, had settled in Vermilion County in its youth. They had been strong abolitionists and devout Presbyterians. The Whitlocks had instilled in their son Hardy an unflinching respect for the law of God and man.

Whitlock had left school at age thirteen to become a farm laborer. He had later worked at a hotel livery and as foreman of a sale stable and livery. In 1888 he came to Danville and ran Lamm's Livery and Feed at 40 North Hazel Street. A strong, well-liked individual, Whitlock became a constable in the city in 1893. The experience he obtained in this position served him well when he became Sheriff.

When Runyan brought the rig to the front of the jail the Sheriff joined him and the two left Danville for Marshfield. Both men were armed with revolvers. As they left the jail, a number of men went inside to inquire about the destination of Whitlock and his deputy.

It was several miles to the small Hoosier village and the road that was most direct led through State Line, Indiana, a town that rested on the Illinois-Indiana border. The rig carrying the two lawmen soon covered the miles as the horse moved at a steady gait. The narrow tracks made by the iron rims of the buggy wheels in the dust of the road were soon wiped out by the prints of other hooves and wheels as people continued to travel to the county seat. When the two lawmen passed through State Line, Indiana, Whitlock was quick to notice the large crowd of men gathered in the city. The crowd did not seem to be a menacing one, but the sight of rifles and shotguns in the hands of many of those standing along the road and talking in small groups, made the Sheriff decide he would not bring his prisoner back this route. He was relieved none of the men followed when they left the village behind.

Back in Danville men continued to gather in small groups at the county jail only to break up and move on when they were told of the capture of a man thought to be the fugitive. Newlin did not have any problem keeping the jail cleared, as most of those who came were merely curious about the manhunt. As the day approached mid afternoon, it began to look like there would be no problems in handling the prisoner. Even with the large number of people in the city, Danville was enjoying a relatively quiet Saturday.

A call came in for the county physician, Doctor Franklin, to go to a residence on North Street where a young woman needed treatment. On going to the residence the physician found the young woman had taken carbonic acid in an attempt to end her life. She told the doctor she was depressed because of an incident that had happened the previous night at a beer party on Gobin Street. Franklin observed that the woman, whose name was Conklin, had only taken a small amount of the acid. He was also aware that the Gobin address, where the party took place, was one of the places that was a constant source of problems for the law. He sternly told the young lady that next time she should take a larger dose of acid and then call an undertaker, not a doctor.

When Whitlock and Runyan arrived in Marshfield, Indiana they found a large crowd gathered about the railroad depot. As Runyan slowed the horse pulling their rig to a walk, the two observed people slowly making room for them to pass. The men here were armed, but as they cradled their weapons in their arms or leaned them against the depot, they did not seem to be in a threatening mood. When the Sheriff asked to be shown the prisoner, he was led into the freight area of the station where Jim Wilson was being guarded by Wurtsbaugh and McHaney. Whitlock thanked the two Hoosiers for their help and told them he would take custody of the prisoner.

The two lawmen walked back to their rig, which was drawn up under a large cottonwood tree, with Wilson between them. There were calls from the crowd, but no one made any attempt to stop the men from taking the prisoner to their buggy. The Sheriff noted the captive seemed to be greatly relieved when they had passed the last house and had left the village of Marshfield behind.

Whitlock observed that Wilson was a large man, though he seemed to be emaciated. His clothing was nearly in shreds and his face and hands were badly scratched from what the Sheriff assumed was his wild run through the fields and woods in an attempt to escape. The lawman could see no evidence that the prisoner had been manhandled in any way by his captors. As the three men made their way back toward Danville, the Sheriff began to question the prisoner.

Wilson told the lawmen he had done nothing wrong. He had been sleeping in an orchard and for no reason two men had taken him into custody. He denied assaulting a woman in Alvin and told his captors he had never been in the town. The young man maintained his innocence as the three slowly made their way back to Danville over the country roads. Whitlock was following a different route than the one he had taken to reach Marshfield. He did not want to risk being waylaid on the way back to the jail by a group of vigilantes.

As the shadows lengthened in the long summer evening, the work week had ended in Vermilion County. The men were now coming into town from the mines, the factories, and the many construction projects that were the mark of a growing city. Streets and sidewalks that had been busy now became crowded with the working men as they made their way into the downtown area.

Many of them were bringing their families to see the free Indian Show which would be taking place in a short while. Others, especially the young men, were seeking out their favorite saloons, which were already beginning to fill.

At the county jail a small group of people still waited for the return of the Sheriff and his prisoner. In the family quarters of the jail, Laura Whitlock was preparing supper for her five children. Her father, who was visiting, would share the evening meal with her and the children. She did not expect her husband to return with his prisoner until dusk. As the County Sheriff's wife it was also her responsibility to help with the feeding of the prisoners. As the people of Danville sat around their tables and enjoyed their evening meals, the individuals that would spark the explosion in the city were drawing closer together.

Whitlock, Runyan, and the prisoner Wilson were nearing Danville as the sun hung in the western sky, a red disc shining through a shroud of humidity. The three men were now covered with a thin layer of gray dust from the long ride on the dirt roads. Wilson had lapsed into a lengthy silence after his initial interrogation and now the Sheriff decided to take another tact with the quiet, young man.

The lawman assumed the prisoner had no idea where they were and he told him they were near the village where the woman had been assaulted. He then asked the man if he would mind if they took him to the home of the woman who had been attacked so she could either identify him or clear him. This proposition brought an immediate response from Wilson. He admitted he had been the one who had been in Alvin. He told the Sheriff he had only entered the Burgess home to find food and he had struck the woman when he was making his escape. He stoutly denied that he intended to harm her in any other way. Whitlock then assured the prisoner, who had been terror stricken at the idea of being taken to the scene of the crime, he would be placed in the county jail in Danville. The three were now passing the first, small frame houses that marked the east edge of the city. In a few minutes they would have their prisoner safely locked up in the county jail.

Chapter Four

Winfield Baker was looking forward to Saturday night as he hitched his horse to a buggy for the short ride into Danville. He had changed from his rough work clothes into a white "Sunday" shirt and dark trousers for his evening outing. With his hair slicked down under his dress up hat, the farm hand climbed into the rig and took the reins in his hand. He was soon on the road heading for the city. In the buggy with him were two revolvers. It was not unusual for men to be armed in 1903 but few of them carried two guns. As the Kentuckian made his way through what was known as the Hungry Hollow neighborhood at the northwest edge of Danville, he saw two of his friends also walking toward the city. He drew his horse up and offered them a ride into Danville. Baker was looking forward to spending some time in Depke's Saloon.

As the three young men made their way through the twilight on the Hungry Hollow Road, the first fire flies of the evening were beginning to twinkle in the deep shade under the trees. A number of other buggies and people walking were also making their way into the city on the narrow dirt road.

Mayor John Beard was working in city hall late on the afternoon of July 25. The Mayor was a man of diverse talents. Among other things he was a master builder. The very building where he was working had been built by his company in 1896. The stone building with its church like steeple, housed police headquarters, the holdover for city prisoners and the police magistrates office on the first floor. The second floor held the council chamber and offices and meeting rooms for city aldermen. Mayor Beard was a staunch Democrat, but he had been elected Mayor three times on the Independent ticket. Beard was a savvy politician and he knew it would be impossible for a Democrat to be elected mayor in the town controlled by the Grand Old Party. Beard's terms had not been consecutive. He was first elected mayor in 1885. He was known as the "Fighting Irishman" because of his spirited approach to situations. He was responsible for the paving of the city's streets and for building a stone arch bridge which connected the east part of the city with the west part. Beard's terms as mayor were all controversial but he would be remembered as being a progressive official. Now, as the Mayor finished his week's work the Sheriff and his prisoner were crossing the very bridge that Beard had built on East Main Street. Destiny was bringing events together and the Mayor would soon be a controversial figure in the historic hours to come.

John W. Keeslar was at his home at 1102 North Vermilion Street on this sultry Saturday evening. Keeslar was the Vermilion County State's Attorney and was highly respected in the legal profession. He was one of the founders of the Vermilion County Bar Association and had taught numerous other young men who became attorneys by taking the law exam. One of his students, Walter Gunn of Danville, became his partner and an Illinois Supreme Court Justice.

Keeslar was of medium height with a slender build. He wore wire rimmed spectacles and his general appearance created the impression of a somewhat meek individual. This was a very misleading conclusion for those to draw who faced the attorney in court. He was a stickler for the letter as well as the intent of the law, and he often inflicted serious legal damage on those who were less informed and capable. He was considered to be a bit quirky by other attorneys because of his fanatic attention to detail. One opposing barrister once commented, after Keeslar had spent what seemed an excessively long period examining a document during a trial, "John has checked for grammatical mistakes, now he will check for content."

The thirty-nine year old prosecutor was also a staunch prohibitionist, did not use profanity, and was not known to have any other vices. An associate observed if he had a sense of humor it was yet to be discovered. Keeslar had received his law degree from the University of Illinois at Bloomington in 1885.

As the State's Attorney relaxed with his wife and daughter in their large Victorian home on North Vermilion Street, the Sheriff was arriving at the jail with his prisoner on South Vermilion. Many of the residents of the "north end," the area where Keeslar lived, were walking downtown to see the free western show that was to take place in the city square.

The area of Danville where John Metcalf lived on Hays Street was far different from that of the Victorian houses on North Vermilion. Small frame buildings with thin walls crowded each other, as if space were at a premium, on the street the construction worker called home. Metcalf had returned home late in the afternoon with his ten dollars pay in his pocket. He had changed from his work clothes into a pair of dark pants and a white shirt. He slipped a jacket over his shirt and before he left his residence he slid a loaded revolver into his inside jacket pocket.

Metcalf left his home and walked slowly toward the saloon area to seek some diversion as the myriad sounds of Saturday night began to echo from the saloons that dotted the downtown area. In a few days his torn, blood stained shirt would be displayed in the window of Gil Fera's restaurant in Chicago. Fera was a former resident of Danville.

Bessie Dodge was also on the street, accompanied by a male acquaintance. She and her companion were walking in the downtown area waiting for the Indian Show to start. As they walked around the city square it was already filling with people, many of them seated on the sidewalk, waiting for the free entertainment to begin. Dodge wore a broad brimmed hat over her red hair, a fact that would be remembered later by a witness to the events yet to come.

At Camp Lincoln, near the state capitol of Springfield, soldiers of the Seventh Regiment of Chicago were training. The unit was also known as the Irish Seventh because of the many men of Irish descent who served in the Seventh. They had earned the name of Fighting Seventh by the recent service of some of the men in the Philippines in the war with Spain. Events that would take place in Danville would cut short the day of rest many of the young men were looking forward to after a hard week in the field.

Governor Richard Yates of Illinois had escaped the heat wave that was baking the state where he served as chief executive. The Governor was summering in Harbor Springs, Michigan and he would spend the next several weeks explaining why he was absent from the state during a time of racial turmoil. A number of Illinois cities had recently been the sight of racial unrest, including Belleville where a man was lynched. In Springfield, Assistant Adjutant Roy Reece was on duty, but he had not been given the authority to take any action in case of emergency.

When Sheriff Whitlock arrived at the jail with his prisoner he found a small group of men waiting on the porch of the brick building. As soon as Deputy Runyan brought the rig to a stop the men left the porch and walked to the buggy to meet the three dusty men. Whitlock jumped to the ground and was followed by the prisoner, Wilson. The captive was looking apprehensively at the approaching men as Whitlock grasped him by the arm and led him toward the jail.

Deputy Newlin came onto the porch and the men made way for the Sheriff and his prisoner as they climbed the steps and walked across the porch. After Whitlock had entered the jail with Wilson, deputies Newlin and Runyan asked the onlookers to leave the area of the jail. The men began to drift away and Deputy Runyan climbed back into the rig and took it across the street to Leonard's Livery.

Inside the jail Laura Whitlock greeted her husband and served him his late supper. She also took food to Jim Wilson after he was placed in a cell. She would remark later that the captive seemed to be nearly starved.

A murmur was running through the cells in the jail as darkness began to embrace the city. The other prisoners were letting it be known that they did not feel safe in a jail that held the man who had assaulted the Alvin woman. Whitlock reassured the captives they were safe and told them none of them were going to be moved or turned loose because of their fears. After the lawman had finished his supper he went to the porch of the jail to visit with his young children who were playing there. The front of the jail was clear now. Most of the people were at the square or seeking entertainment somewhere else.

As the tired Sheriff relaxed on the porch of his jail it appeared it might be a normal Saturday night in Danville. Loud voices and laughter could be heard from Shaffer's Saloon, just up the street from the jail, but these sounds were softened by the chirping of crickets as they performed their nightly summer symphony. As the

Whitlock family enjoyed the last light of the long summer evening the fuse for the coming explosion was about to be lit on East Main Street.

Chapter Five

Shermayer's Saloon was filled with the Saturday night crowd. The long narrow building which fronted East Main was a popular drinking place for the large German population of the area. Working behind the bar was Charles Shermayer, a saloon keeper who had the reputation of running a peaceful enterprise. But it was no accident that Shermayer's had a minimum of trouble in a city noted for its rowdiness. In a rack behind the well polished bar, within easy reach of Shermayer or his bar men, hung a twelve gauge shotgun with the barrel sawed off. Customers knew the owner did not hesitate to bounce those who created problems.

Standing at the bar with his friends, their faces looking back at them from the mirror that hung behind the bar, was Henry Carl Gatterman. The butcher had gone to his home at 828 Bowman Avenue following work and changed out of his meat cutter's clothes. He had then returned to Shermayer's. Since he became engaged to Hazel Smith, he had not spent many Saturday nights with his old friends. Now, with his bride-to-be visiting family out of town, the young German was spending the evening with some of them. Gatterman was waiting on Harley Croucher, but he did not see Croucher in the crowded saloon. After visiting a short time longer, he left the saloon to go in search of his friend.

John Metcalf was walking east on East Main Street He had just crossed the Wabash Railroad tracks and was nearing Shermayer's Saloon. The construction worker had walked to the downtown area, now he was on his way back toward Hays Street where he lived. As he continued east, Metcalf noticed two men approching him.

When Gatterman walked out of Shermayer's, he found Harley

Croucher was just arriving. The two men exchanged greetings, then Gatterman suggested they walk to the square and watch the free western show that would soon begin. The two men started to walk west on East Main toward the city square. They had only gone a few steps when they met John Metcalf at the northwest corner of Main and McDonald. Though it was a Saturday night, the three were the only ones on the sidewalk at the moment.

As Metcalf approached the pair he thought he recognized one of them. The construction worker called out to Harley Croucher, "Are you the man who called me a Nigger when you passed my house awhile ago?" Croucher informed him that he had made no such remark.

Metcalf then turned to Gatterman and asked if he was the one who had made the remark. The meat cutter also denied that he was the one who had called out to Metcalf. The two men then became engaged in an argument. As their voices were raised, a few people who were approaching on the nearly deserted sidewalk stopped to watch. Harley Croucher also backed away from the two as they closed in on each other.

Now the two were heatedly arguing over who should make way for the other on the sidewalk. Metcalf placed his hand on the inside of his coat and quickly closed the distance between himself and Gatterman. The young German was not as large as the construction worker, but he was muscular, and now he stepped forward and struck Metcalf with a blow to the face which knocked the man back some distance and caused him to stagger. Metcalf quickly recovered and pulled a revolver from his coat. He once again approached Gatterman, this time with the pistol thrust out in front of him.

Gatterman did not back away and the two men struggled, both men grasping the revolver that Metcalf had pulled. Now a large crowd was beginning to gather and many of the onlookers were standing in the street. No one made a move to stop the fight as the two men clasped each other and Gatterman tried to obtain the revolver.

Then the larger Metcalf was able to push the meat cutter's arms upward and he thrust his weapon against Gatterman's left breast. As the two men faced each other Metcalf squeezed the trigger of his gun and there was a loud explosion as he sent a bullet into Gatterman's chest.

It was noisy in Shermayer's Saloon but the sound of a gun shot only a few feet from the front door penetrated the din of the bar. Charles Shermayer pushed his way through the men who were crowding out the door to see what had happened. The saloon keeper had to make his way through a large circle of people on the outside of his business who were watching the fight. He then saw Gatterman and Metcalf struggling for a gun held by Metcalf. There was bright blood streaming from the smaller man's mouth. Shermayer turned and ran back into the saloon for his shotgun.

When Shermayer came running back out with a shotgun in his hands the people quickly cleared away, many of them knew what a scatter-gun could do. He approached the two men and brought the shotgun up to cover Metcalf. As soon as the saloon keeper had a clear shot at the construction worker he pulled the trigger. There was a metallic click and it was then that he remembered he had failed to load the gun. Metcalf now moved the wounded Gatterman between himself and the man with the shotgun. But the butcher was still putting up a strong struggle despite his wound, and Metcalf was unable to handle him and watch Shermayer at the same time.

The saloon man now struck Metcalf a glancing blow with his gun. As the construction worker moved to avoid the full force of the blow, he brought his revolver up and fired two quick shots at Shermayer. The shots did not hit their target but one of the bullets did wound bystander Ed Burkwalder. The crowd ran for cover as the shots were fired by Metcalf.

Gatterman was now rapidly loosing his strength. He still clung to the larger man but his life's blood had already turned his shirt red. Metcalf now placed his revolver against the young German's shoulder and fired a second shot into him. Gatterman released his hold on Metcalf and began to stagger away, once again walking west toward the square. He would never see the Indian Show he had planned on going to just a few minutes before.

As Metcalf fired his shot into Gatterman he was struck by a blow from Shermayer's gun with such force that the stock of the gun shattered. The construction worker began to run east on Main, but he was slowed down by the blow he had received on the back from Shermayer. As Metcalf ran, he still clutched his pistol in his hand. The construction worker was followed closely by Harley Croucher. Now several other men joined in the chase and a call was put in to the police station on Walnut Street to send a wagon.

Officer William Leverenz was walking a beat on East Main when he thought he heard a shot. He soon heard the other shots fired by Metcalf, and the veteran Danville police officer began to run east toward the sound of the trouble. As he neared the scene of the shooting, he saw a man leaning against the wall of Miller's Bakery. It took him a moment to recognize the ashen face of Henry Gatterman in the twilight of the evening. The two men were good friends. Gatterman's mother had married John Leverenz after her husband died and the dying man had made his home with his stepfather.

Leverenz asked Gatterman what had happened, but the man only replied "Will, this is my last." The officer could see that there was no hope for his friend. As other people had arrived, including Gatterman's cousin, he left them with him and continued to run east in search of the mortally wounded man's assailant. There were other people running east with Leverenz and he could hear shouts coming from the direction in which he was going.

Officer William Foehrer was working the beat east of the one covered by Leverenz. He, like Leverenz, was a veteran of Saturday night trouble in Danville. Foehrer also heard the sound of gunshots, and he began to move toward the sound from the opposite direction of Leverenz. Foehrer drew his revolver as he ran. In the distance he could see a number of men speeding in his direction. The streetlights were now on and shadows chased the running men as they raced through the humid air of the evening.

John Metcalf could hardly run, due to the crushing blow from Shermayer's shotgun on his back. He knew the man he had been fighting was finished, now he had to try to get away. He was only a block from the street where he lived. He could have ran north on McDonald Street and cut across North Street but he had decided to run east on Main. As he ran, he found that his legs did not seem to want to work right. The blow he had received on his back had done something to him. He was able to manage a trot but he found that he was being closely followed by a number of men who had watched the fight. Though he had been drinking, Metcalf was not drunk. He clutched his weapon tighter in his hand as he approached Hays Street. In the gloom ahead he could see a police officer approaching with his revolver drawn.

Metcalf made the turn and slowly began to run north on Hays, he would soon be home. Foehrer saw the man with the gun clearly as he made the turn from East Main onto Hays. The officer was closing the distance between the two of them and was able to cut between the man and a group who were pursuing him. The race was soon over. Foehrer called out for the man to throw down his weapon and to raise his hands. Metcalf did as he was told. He stood quietly as the officer walked up to him and picked up the revolver he had thrown on the ground.

Before Foehrer could ask any questions, Harley Croucher came running up, closely followed by William Leverenz and a number of others. Leverenz and Foehrer exchanged knowing looks and both drew their billy clubs. They then placed Metcalf between them and told the growing crowd of men and boys that were gathering around them to back up. As the police officers and their prisoner began to make their way south on Hays to Main, the body of Henry Gatterman was being picked up to be taken to the mortuary. From the crowd that followed the officers, an ominous word was being repeated, "Lynch, Lynch, Lynch."

In the police station at city hall Captain Obediah Phillips was in command of the night shift. He was on duty when a call came in from East Main reporting that a black man had shot a white man during a fight. The caller said the man who had done the shooting was being chased and a paddy wagon was needed at Shermayer's Saloon. The call ended any thoughts of a normal Saturday night. Captain Phillips told an officer to bring a wagon around, he would make the run himself. A shooting of this nature would cause problems on any night, but Phillips was well aware of what it could cause on Saturday night. The saloons and honky tonks were already well filled and by now a number of their customers had been drinking for hours. Phillips was aware of the lynchings that had taken place in the past few weeks in Belleville, Illinois and Evansville, Indiana. While it seemed unlikely that such a thing could occur in Danville, there were people with deep racial prejudices in the city. The shooting could cause major problems for the law.

Phillips drove his wagon east on North Street as rapidly as he dared with people crossing the street and other vehicles moving through the intersections. It was about six blocks to Shermayer's and the officer noted there was a large number of people on the city's thoroughfares. The heat and humidity had evidently caused many of them to leave their homes in search of a cool breeze. It only took him a few minutes to reach the saloon and he saw a crowd of men, women, and young boys gathered on the street as he approached the west side of Shermayer's building. He pulled his wagon up near a telephone pole on McDonald Street and jumped down to see if the wanted man was in the crowd.

Foehrer and Leverenz moved their prisoner as quickly as they could down Hays Street. Though they had warned the growing crowd around them to stay back, men and young boys were still darting close to them and shouting taunts at their prisoner, then darting back into the crowd. The procession soon turned the corner and walked west on Main. The officers were looking for a paddy wagon and reinforcements.

When they reached the area near Shermayer's where the trouble had started they saw the paddy wagon coming down McDonald Street. The two officers backed up against the wall of the building with their prisoner and waited on the police vehicle to reach them. Every occupant of Shermayer's had now joined the crowd pressing in on the two officers.

As Captain Phillips made his way through the people, he saw Leverenz and Foehrer standing against the wall with a large man between them. The command officer shouted at the people to make way and the three lawmen moved the prisoner to the wagon. As they started to load Metcalf into the horse drawn vehicle, a number of men surged forward from the circle of onlookers. Foehrer and Leverenz struck a number of well aimed blows with their nightsticks and some men went down while the others fell back. Metcalf was then loaded for the trip to the city jail. Through the whole experience the handcuffed captive showed little fear.

As the hooves of the horse began to beat out their rhythmic sound on the paving bricks of the street, they were accompanied by the sound of running feet Most of the crowd from Shermayer's was following the wagon to the jail, and as they ran they were shouting "Lynch! Lynch! Lynch!"

Chapter Six

Whitlock was still on the porch with his children when a figure came running down the street toward the jail. He recognized one of his deputies as the breathless man hurried up the steps to where the Sheriff was sitting. "All hell's going to break loose!" the excited man exclaimed.

Then he filled the Sheriff in on what he knew of the events that had just occurred on East Main. The deputy ended by telling Whitlock that men were on their way to the city jail to get the prisoner and lynch him.

Whitlock knew about lynching and he knew about duty. He had been a constable in May of 1895 when the last lynching in Vermilion County took place. He had already stated that none of his prisoners would be lynched as long as he were alive to protect them.

In 1895 a man and a teenage boy, both white, had been taken into custody for allegedly assaulting a young girl. Sheriff Thompson had arrested them and was holding them in the county jail for trial. On the night of May 24th a mob of about a thousand, led by the girl's father, had broken in the door of the jail with an iron rail and taken the two men out. It had all been quiet and business-like. The Sheriff had asked the mob to disperse but they ignored him. Judge Bookwalter had also told the mob to let the law take its course, but his pleas fell on deaf ears. The Sheriff stood aside while his prisoners were taken from the jail and marched to the Gilbert Street Bridge. There they had nooses placed around their necks and were thrown over the side of the bridge.

Whitlock had seen the still bodies, swinging on their ropes, the morning after their three A.M. lynching. He also knew that there was considerable doubt as to the guilt of the teenager. The men's names were William Royce and John Halls, Jr. Whitlock also remembered what Sheriff Thompson had said about his defense of the prisoners. "We resisted as best we could but it would have taken a regiment to hold the crowd back."

The Sheriff now sent his children inside, and with deputies Newlin and Runyan, started for city hall, which was a block west and two blocks north of the county jail. The three men carried revolvers as they strode purposely toward the city lockup. When they reached Walnut Street, the lawmen found people running toward the stone city building from all directions. The Indian Show they had just passed on the city square was still holding the attention of a large audience, but events on Walnut Street would soon prove to be a bigger draw.

Captain Phillips traced the same route he had taken from the police station to Shermayer's on his return trip to city hall. He was conscious that there were a lot of men following him. He also knew word of the arrest on East Main would soon spread throughout the downtown area. Phillips was not surprised to see a number of people already at the jail when he pulled up in the alley beside the station. He, Leverenz, and Foeher quickly moved Metcalf from the paddy wagon to the interior of the jail. Once inside Metcalf had his handcuffs removed and was placed in a cell. A number of patrol officers were on hand and Phillips ordered them to secure the building, only authorized persons would be permitted inside.

The jailer who placed Metcalf in his cell asked the construction worker if he knew the name of the man he had shot. The prisoner replied that he did not. He was then told by the turn key that he would most likely be lynched. "Well, it can't be helped," Metcalf answered. "It will be just one more dead nigger."

The crowd in front of city hall was growing larger by the minute. What had been only a scattering of people had quickly turned into a gathering of at least two hundred. As the sound of the crowd grew louder, there was a knock on the locked front door of the building. An officer looked out and saw Whitlock and his two deputies standing before the door. The three lawmen were admitted and the Sheriff told Phillips they would render help in any way he wanted it.

There was growing concern on the inside of the jail for the safety of the prisoner. It was decided he should be hidden, and Metcalf was removed from his common cell and taken to the vault in the basement of the building. The jailer locked his prisoner in the small room and returned to the main floor. Metcalf was the only captive being held at city hall.

What had once been a crowd had now turned into a mob of more than a thousand people around the city building. Voices were calling for the prisoner to be turned over and some members of the mob were beginning to press forward toward the front door of city hall. The participants were mainly men, but there was a sprinkling of women and young boys mixed in. Some of the younger women were being ordered away by family members as the intentions of the leaders of the assemblage became more apparent.

A number of men now went to the front steps of city hall and attempted to quiet the mob. They were quickly hooted and hissed into silence by the still growing mob that was pushing steadily closer to the building. The roar of their voices could be heard for several blocks, and the Indian Show was coming to an early end on the square. The men then told the mob they had been deputized to help keep order at city hall but this bit of news was also ignored by the milling mass of people who were edging closer to the building that held Metcalf.

There were a number of armed city police inside city hall and those in charge decided to send some of them to the north side of the building to form a picket line. It was felt that the north door would be the most vulnerable to attack by the mob. When the uniformed officers filed from the jail and spaced themselves across the alley to prevent access to the building, they became the objects of the mob's wrath. As the solid wave of humanity shoved its way toward the thin line of uniformed officers, the police pulled their revolvers.

Inside the jail Hardy Whitlock waited for instructions, but none came. He and his two men remained standing near the front door of the jail, an occasional glance out a window showed the mob to be gaining strength by the minute. Whitlock realized he was sitting on a powder keg. While there was only one prisoner, Metcalf, in the city building, the county jail had a number of men in its cells. Among them were two men arrested for murder, as well as Jim Wilson, who had been charged with the assault on the Burgess woman. As the calls for a lynching gained greater intensity there were also racial remarks being hurled at the defenders.

In the windowless basement vault of the jail, John Metcalf waited in darkness. The sounds from the street penetrated the walls that held him prisoner, but no light found its way into the small room that opened off the area where the police stored their equipment. Metcalf's jacket had been removed when he was arrested, he had been told it would be returned to him later. As the construction worker huddled in a corner of the small room, the building vibrated as something struck it a sharp blow.

The police in line on the north side of city hall waited for orders. Only a few yards separated them from the mob, and as they watched, the distance was shrinking. The officers glanced nervously at the door of the jail, waiting for a command officer to appear. They knew their mere presence in the dark alley was not going to deter the hundreds of people who were pressing towards them. They leveled their weapons at the foremost figures in the mob, and the two groups seemed frozen for a few seconds. Then the mob surged forward like a single living thing, and struck the line of police.

The officers were first shoved back and then pushed to the ground, their weapons taken from them by dozens of rough hands. The alley became so full of men crowding toward the door of the jail that there was no place for them to move. Then a voice called out to make way and a number of men came forward with a ten foot section of streetcar rail.

Individuals were shoved aside and a narrow path was cleared in front of the wooden door on the north side of city hall. Like a pendulum, the men began to swing the battering ram back and forth. When it had gained momentum, they sent it slamming into the door of the city building. A loud cry of approval went up from the mob when they heard the rail strike the door. A number of men now held torches above their heads to provide light in the alley.

The blow from the battering ram jarred the defenders on the inside of the jail into action. Whitlock and his deputies drew their weapons and the city officers readied their night sticks. Then word was passed around that there was to be no shooting. The lawmen with drawn guns put them away and all eyes were focused on the north door of the jail. They were rewarded with a series of strong thuds as the ram struck relentlessly against the unyielding oak. On the wall of the station hung a loaded riot gun, but no one made a move to take it down from its pegs. From the outside of the building a cheer went up each time the iron rail struck the door.

When Whitlock saw the first cracks appear in the north door of the jail, he moved his deputies toward the door that opened onto Walnut Street. The lawman could see what was coming in a few seconds. Even as the three moved to the east door, the ram burst through the north door in a shower of splintering wood. The ruined door was quickly knocked off its hinges, and the men who had filled the alley rushed into the breech in the building's security. A brief struggle broke out as the police tried to hold the men back. Officers Lopp, Leverenz, and Stith were knocked to the floor and injured as the building filled with the mob. Then all resistance to the rioters ceased. The building was no longer in the hands of the law.

Whitlock saw that all was lost at the city building. He opened the door and was leaving when one of those who had entered the building called out to him. The man told the Sheriff they would be paying him a visit as soon as they had finished their work at the jail. Whitlock assured the man the mob would receive a little warmer welcome at the county jail than it had received in the building they were presently occupying. Then the grim faced lawman, followed by his two deputies, left the doomed building and headed back to the county jail.

The three lawmen had to push their way through the throngs of people gathered in front of the jail. They found the mob extended almost a block south of the building. When they reached the town square it was nearly deserted. What people were on the street were walking toward the roar that was coming from city hall. As they walked by the saloons that were normally full, they noticed the watering holes were nearly empty. The patrons were now a part of the lawless horde that was wrecking city hall. When the three walked onto the porch of the county jail they could still hear the sounds of the mob in the distance. The sound was lower now, like the distant rumble of thunder in a gathering summer storm.

Chapter Seven

A black man walking down Walnut Street from the north came to the edge of the mob and at once drew the attention of those nearest him. He was quickly told that he was in a bad place by a police officer, and that he should make himself scarce. The man turned and started running east on North Street. But members in the rear of the large crowd did not know their quarry was still in the jail. They were standing on North, around the corner and half a block distant from the city building. When the man came running past, a cry went up that their man was escaping. Blows were struck as he ran past and a chase began. It was a short race and the man was caught at the Aetna Hotel corner, a block east of city hall. He had already been injured by the mob when a police officer stepped forward and told those beating him that the man they wanted was still in the city building. The unfortunate passerby was released by those holding him and he limped away. The mob members who had assaulted him ran back to join those at city hall

Mayor Beard was told of the successful storming of city hall and was asked to take steps to curb the violence. He told the police to close the saloons. The last thing a mob like the one now gathered needed was a ready source of alcohol. When word was taken around to the saloon keepers, they at once rebelled. Saturday night was their big night of the week and it was not yet nine in the evening. Police informed the Mayor of the saloon keepers refusal and he sent the officers back to the drinking establishments with word that they be closed by 10 P.M.

City hall was filled with hundreds of members of the mob. They had been told by the police that the man they were seeking was not in the building. They found the door to the cell block was locked, and the battering ram was brought in and the door was knocked in. As the frenzied men found cell after cell empty they turned their fury on the building. Windows were knocked out, furniture was broken, and every door was knocked in and destroyed. When the search was completed on the first floor of the building, without any success, mob members crowded up the stairs to the council chambers and offices. Here they continued their pattern of destruction, becoming more violent as they once again met with failure in their search for the prisoner. A number of men were boosted into the building's attic where they used lanterns to search the dark recesses. Those without a light quickly came crashing down through the plaster and lath ceiling into the council chambers. Several of the vigilantes were injured in the wild search.

Metcalf still crouched in the corner of the vault in the basement of the building. The sounds of breaking doors and furniture, and the maddened shouts and curses of the mob, were very near now. The construction worker was not only a prisoner, he was in a trap, one from which there was no escape. When he had pulled the trigger on his gun and shot Gatterman, he had almost certainly guaranteed himself a trip to the gallows that waited for murderers in the county jail building. But the sound of footfalls approaching the door of the vault where he was hidden let him know that death was much nearer than a sheriff's gallows.

The men who went to the basement of the jail tried the door to the vault but they found it locked. Word was sent up the stairs that the rail was needed and in a few moments the streetcar iron was being maneuvered into the area in front of the locked door. The vault door proved more of a challenge than had the doors on the first floor. The men swinging the rail were soaked with sweat by the time the door broke free of its lock and swung halfway open. A lantern was held up and the rioters looked into the vault.

A triumphant shout went up as the vigilantes saw Metcalf crouching in a corner of the small room. The captive pleaded with the men to leave him alone, but when he saw that was a hopeless request he began to fight the men who crowded into the room. He was a strong man but the fight was soon over. He was carried out of the vault he had been held in, to the stairs that led to the main floor.

When the men packing the upper floors of city hall heard the roar from the basement, they all tried to get downstairs to get to the prisoner. As Metcalf fought his way up the stairs through the packed members of the mob, many of them struck each other in their effort to hit the desperate man. Once the fight reached the main floor of city hall it was soon over. Numerous men fell on Metcalf, one of them striking him with a hammer, another with a piece of gas pipe. When it seemed there was no more fight left in Metcalf, as he lay on the floor, he was picked up by a number of rioters and thrown out one of the broken windows of city hall.

When the mass of people on the outside saw the bloody, unconscious body of Metcalf come flying out the window of Danville's municipal building, a triumphant roar split the air. A number of people crowded around to kick the body when it hit the ground, others went in search of a rope. A man soon came running up with a rope he had secured at Joe Long's feed yard and it was deftly tied around Metcalf's neck. A cry went up to hang the beaten man but other's shouted they wanted to take him back to Shermayer's where the shooting of Gatterman had taken place.

There was only a moment's hesitation, and then, like a leaderless army, the great mass of people began to move east on North Street. Willing hands grasped the rope and Metcalf was dragged over the paving bricks, his body being kicked, beaten, and spit on every step of the way.

The procession passed in front of the offices of the *Danville Democrat* at 18 West North and the *Commercial-News* at 17 West North. Workers for the two papers watched the rioters passing by and their reporters followed along, scribbling notes on their pads. It was the beginning of press coverage that would reach every major paper in the country and would maintain people's interest for weeks to come. Horses and buggies drew up and moved to the sides of the street as the mob approached them, the buggy lamps adding illumination to the improbable scene of lawlessness in the county seat.

At the intersection of North and Vermilion, the patrons of the Aetna Hotel came out to watch the dark scene. An out of town client of a Danville attorney promptly became ill when he saw the battered and bloody form of Metcalf being pulled along in front of the procession. Earlier he had remarked to the lawyer that nothing much ever happened in Danville. The men and women standing in front of the Aetna, resplendent in their evening dress, would never forget the scene passing before their eyes. Just three blocks north of the intersection was the home of Joseph G. Cannon, Speaker of the United States House of Representatives. Uncle Joe, as he was known to his constituents, would be livid with anger when word reached him of the rioting in Danville.

The sounds of the riot penetrated far north on Vermilion Street where Victorian mansions fronted the street under towering elms. People from the north end began to drift downtown to "see the excitement." One who didn't was State's Attorney Keeslar. There would be numerous reports from people, some from eyewitnesses years after the historic night, that Keeslar spoke to the crowd, but the slender attorney remained in his home. His work would come later.

It was nearly half a mile from city hall to Shermayer's Saloon, and the mob grew in size as it marched along. At some point, as his bloodied head bounced over the rough bricks of the street, life left the broken body of John Metcalf. But those who pulled it along as a prize did not seem satisfied that their vigilante style justice had been carried out, they were out of control. A blood lust seemed to have fallen over many of the rioters and it was yet to be satisfied.

In the county jail on South Vermilion, Sheriff Hardy Whitlock was readying his deputies for what must come. The broad shouldered man looked forbidding as his large mustache seemed to droop even more than usual in the steamy July night. He had sent his wife and children to their living quarters on the second floor of the jail. The lawman exchanged a few words with his father-in-law, then he put on a dark hat and opened the door and walked onto the porch of his jail. Word had been received that there was a large group from the Alvin area coming to try to remove Jim Wilson from the jail. These rumors would prove to be false, but the sound of breaking glass and the howling of the mob in the distance left the Sheriff with little doubt as to where the rioters would end up. The street in front of the jail remained empty as the lawman waited for events to develop. In the distance, trains could be heard passing through the city, their whistles muted hauntingly in the heavy air.

A few city blocks distant from the brick, county jail building, the rioters had at last reached their destination on McDonald Street. Metcalf had arrived at the same spot for the third time this evening, his lifeless body lay beside the utility pole that Captain Phillips had pulled the paddy wagon up to a short time earlier. Only a few feet away were the blood stains from Henry Gatterman's fatal wounds. As the lawless horde milled around, a man quickly tossed the rope tied to Metcalf's neck over a cross arm on the pole. Then a number of men grasped the rope and pulled the lynching victim clear of the ground. The rope was then made fast and the body was suspended in the heavy night air. As Metcalf's sightless eyes stared back at them, a number of men pulled revolvers and began shooting at the body. One of the bullets struck a bystander and the crowd drew back from the area. A reporter scribbled down the wounded man's name as Otto Heinke. But what he had heard was that the wounded man was being taken to Otto Heinke's place of business, East End Drug, to await an ambulance. The name of the injured rioter was never known.

As the body of John Metcalf slowly turned on the lynch rope, the men put their revolvers away. The mob still showed no indication that it was satisfied with what it had accomplished. Then someone suggested that the body should be thrown in the Vermilion River. This met with a roar of approval and Metcalf was taken down from the pole. But as the rioters began to drag the corpse in the direction of the river, others began to shout that it should be burned. This seemed an even better idea to the throng that was near enough to hear the suggestions and the procession was halted as men began to look for kindling for a fire. Then Winfield Baker stepped forward and called out in a loud voice. "Let's get the Alvin Nigger!"

For a moment the noise of the mob seemed to ebb. They had forgotten the prisoner in the county jail in the excitement of lynching Metcalf. A few of the rioters had suggested going to the bottoms and burning the entire black community, but as yet no one had moved in that direction. Now Baker had given them a new target to vent their rage upon.

"On to the jail, on to the jail!" The cry was picked up by hundreds of voices and once again the human mass began to move. In the lead was a line of men pulling the body of Metcalf behind them, the battered head staining Danville's Main Street. There were now a number of individuals in the mob who were hopelessly drunk and others were fast becoming that way. As the wild horde of people made its way toward the county jail, rocks were thrown through store windows along their route. In the forefront of the mob was the tall figure of the Kentuckian, Winfield Baker, two pistols resting securely in his belt. As the rioters left Shermayer's a small fire began to flicker in the middle of McDonald Street. So huge was the mob that some members were of the opinion that the lynching victim was still to be burned at the Saloon. When they saw they were being left behind, they threw down the packing boxes they were making into kindling and ran to join the other rioters.

Street lights gave a dim radiance to the spectacle that was passing down Danville's Main Street. The hot steamy night had brought many families from their homes, and now they observed the grisly parade passing in front of them.

Railroad workers and train crews were on hand to see the handiwork of the mob as the rioters moved off, dragging Metcalf's body like a captured trophy. The railroad men quickly spread the word to the train stations in the city and word was passed up and down the line by the telegraphers: RIOTING IN DANVILLE!

Young boys, many of them in bare feet, ran wildly along side the rioters. Men in silk hats and silk shirts with break away collars marched beside miners in their coarse work clothes and miner's caps. Almost every head in the sea of moving people was covered with some sort of headgear. Slouch hats, derbies, narrow brimmed straw hats, and all manner of work caps were worn by the men as they moved rapidly toward the county jail. The women bobbed along wearing everything from hats that appeared to be topped by a bouquet of flowers, to day bonnets which suggested they might not have been home since afternoon. Conspicuously absent from the mass of moving people were young girls, they had been kept or sent home.

As the sounds of the approaching mob echoed down Vermilion Street to the jail, Whitlock decided it was time to ask for outside help to deal with the mob. He felt he was facing a situation that he lacked the means to deal with. The Sheriff sent a deputy to the Western Union office with a message to be telegraphed to the Governor in Springfield. The telegraph office of Western Union was located at 115 N. Vermilion, and as Deputy Newlin made his way up the street the mob was already approaching the square.

Whitlock now went to the upstairs of the jail building and told Laura to take their children and move to a safer place. She refused and told him she was staying with him and would not send the children away. Whitlock pleaded with her to go, explaining the building would soon be under siege, but she remained adamant in her refusal. As the sounds from the mob grew louder, the Sheriff gave in and left his family and returned to the downstairs of the jail. He could hear a new sound now, the prisoners were praying in their cells.

The mob was so huge that it broke into two separate parts, one portion would approach the jail from the north on Vermilion Street, the other section would come from the east on South Street. As the pace of the rioters quickened, they passed the men dragging the remains of Metcalf. Some of the leaders now began to break into a run as they neared the jail. All wanted to be first to drag the next prisoner from his cell.

At city hall the police were regrouping and debating what to do next. A number of them had been injured in the brief fight when their building was overrun. Others had been hurt by stones hurled at them by the mob. Those who were able were sent back out on normal patrol, others were being called in to help with what might develop later. There was no help sent to the county jail.

As the rioters gathered around the county jail a telegram was going over the wires to Springfield:

Governor Richard Yates,
Hurry militia if possible / trouble
condition affair. unable to cope
with situation
H.H.
Whitlock, Sheriff

The wire would reach a city without a governor and no one present had the authority to handle an emergency. While Whitlock was waiting for an answer to his call for aid, Governor Richard Yates was enjoying the cool weather in Harbor Springs, Michigan.

The street was no longer empty in front of the county jail building. One of the largest masses of people ever assembled in the city of Danville now packed the street. So huge was the crowd that it was backed up a block north on Vermilion and two blocks east on South Street. The rioters presented a savage appearance as they began to face their next target, many of them were armed with clubs, pitchforks, and axes. Others brandished revolvers as they shouted at the top of their lungs, "Lynch! Lynch! Lynch!"

Then the mob parted a few feet to make a path for the men dragging the body of Metcalf to its next destination. The limp form of the lynching victim was placed at the northeast corner of South and Vermilion. The battered body was clad only in a tattered pair of pants. Metcalf's shoes, socks, and shirt had been torn off during his beating. Now a man stepped forward and cut the rope from the neck of the corpse and carefully wound it into neat loops. Pieces would be sold for souvenirs in the next few days.

A few of the rioters disappeared inside of Hartman's Livery at 101 South Vermilion and soon reappeared carrying bundles of straw. The straw was placed next to the body and when the pile had reached a suitable height the remains of Metcalf were thrown on top of the golden straw. A torch was then touched to the work and the pyre began to blaze brightly in the sultry night. A cheer went up from those near enough to see as the flames began to touch the broken form on top of the fire. One of those helping with the burning was a man named Mitchell. He would be haunted by the face of Metcalf for years after the lynching every time he looked into the blazing coals in his furnace.

Chapter Eight

When Danville's city hall had been overrun by the mob it had been a leaderless, spontaneous action. The horde facing the county building was better organized. Winfield Baker and a few others had formed a committee to search the jail for Jim Wilson and two other prisoners. They had decided the lynching of three more men would finish their night's work.

Now Baker accosted Constable Enoch VanVickle as the officer made his way to the jail. VanVickle turned when he heard the Kentuckian call out to him. As Baker walked up he held his two revolvers in his hands, but he did not threaten the lawman with them. In a low tone he told VanVickle he needed the keys to the jail or he would like to have three prisoners turned over to him. He gave the names of the three men the mob had condemned to death. VanVickle told the Kentuckian the prisoners were where they were supposed to be and that was where they would stay. Baker then pointed to the blazing fire that was scorching the body on the curb. He informed the Constable if he and the others had to storm the jail, no quarter would be given to any of the prisoners or defenders. He told VanVickle to take a good look if that was how he wanted to end up. Baker then turned and walked back to a small group of men who had been earnestly listening to the conversation. He told them it was time to knock the streetlights out.

Whitlock called his small band of defenders together. In the building that was now an island surrounded by the hostile crowd, they were deputies Charles Runyan, David Newlin, Frank Wrisk, Peter O'Brien, John Steward, and Constable VanVickle. As they were discussing strategy there was a knock on the barred door of the jail, and Special Agent for the Wabash Railroad, John Seward, asked admittance. The detective was let into the jail and he offered his services to the embattled Sheriff. Also on hand was Laura Whitlock's father. The former provost marshal from Indiana was also given a weapon. The Sheriff told the men he was going to try to calm the mob, but that under no circumstance were they to be allowed to set foot in the jail. He looked intently at each one of them and instructed them to let him do the shooting if it came to that. The others were only to use their weapons if "the worst" came. During the meeting Laura Whitlock and the children came down the stairs and were listening to the conversation. Now the small woman asked to be given a gun. Whitlock told her to return upstairs and watch the children, that he and the deputies could handle things. Then the Sheriff went to the door of the jail and opened it to the thunderous noise of the mob.

Word had spread rapidly of the rioting in Danville. In 1903 nearly every small town had a railway station. Many medium sized villages had two stations if there were two rail lines passing through the town. The stations were tied together by telegraph wires that would sing out the news of events up and down the line.

On the night of July 25th, telegraphers were busily tapping out the story of the rioting in Danville. The news went out over the lines of the Wabash, the C&EI, and the Big Four railroads. Before the mob ever reached the county jail on South Vermilion Street, reporters from newspapers as far away as Chicago and St. Louis were making arrangements for transportation to the county seat of Vermilion County, Illinois.

In Chicago, a man with more than a passing interest in the affair received word of the rioting. He was Vermilion County Circuit Judge Morton W. Thompson. When the Judge received news of the violence that was occurring in his home town, he sent word that he would return on the first train available. He lived on Pine Street only two blocks from the devastated city hall.

Thompson was a tough individual, but was considered to be a fair man when he put on his judicial robes. He was born near the small Vermilion County village of Fithian in 1858. His home stood on the Old State Road and as a child he had watched the last of the prairie schooners as they passed the farm on their way west. Thompson had wanted to be an attorney early in his youth and had been encouraged in his pursuit of the law by his younger brother, John.

The brother would become one of the great success stories of American business during the era by establishing the first national restaurant chain. Thompson was also influenced by the fact that Abraham Lincoln had been a friend of his father. The rail splitter had stayed at the Thompson farm when he rode the circuit.

Thompson, like State's Attorney Keeslar, had been one of the founders of the Vermilion County Bar Association. He had also served a brief time as state's attorney before he was appointed judge. While many considered State's Attorney Keeslar to be a tedious individual in the courtroom, they had an entirely different opinion of Mort Thompson. The Judge was a no-nonsense man who did not believe in "hog-tying the law with a lot of legal shenanigans."

Another individual in the Windy City had also been personally affected by news from Danville. Hazel Smith had received word of the death of Henry Carl Gatterman. The distraught young woman was making arrangements to return to Danville for the services. There would be no wedding for her in the autumn.

As the wires spread the word up and down the line, they also sent a message for the fast passenger train that was to stop in Alvin. The south bound train was given an order to proceed through the town without making its regular stop. There was fear a mob was waiting near the station to board the train for Danville. When the C&EI passenger train steamed through the small village at full speed, there was no mob waiting, only a number of regular passengers stood at the station watching helplessly as the train left them behind.

In the Illinois capitol, Roy Reece was frantically trying to find someone with the authority to send aid to the embattled Sheriff in Vermilion County. There were state troops available at Camp Lincoln and they could be in Danville in a few hours if an order was secured to send them. But as the assistant adjutant tried to contact those with the authority to handle a crisis situation, he was frustrated at every turn. The governor would not be available until the next day. A wire sent to him would be delivered at his vacation site in Michigan. Lieutenant Governor Northcott was at his home in Greenville, Illinois, but wires sent to that city failed to obtain a response. Adjutant General Thomas W. Scott was at his home near Fairfield, isolated from communications. The man next in the rotation of power was Colonel John S. G. Ogelsby, the governor's private secretary, and no one had a clue as to his location.

Word was sent to the army camp alerting the officers of a possible troop movement, but the men were not given the order to stand to arms. While Reece was searching for one of the elusive state leaders, a second message was being sent over the wires from Danville.

Sheriff Hardy Whitlock walked slowly through the mob, speaking to individuals, pleading with them to go home. No one made any move to harm the lawman as he spoke earnestly about letting the law take its course, but no one seemed to pay him any heed. He saw one individual who he thought would have an impact on the mob, and he asked him to speak to them but the man told him, "God himself couldn't stop this bunch, Hardy." He was then advised to give up the jail and save himself a lot of trouble.

The Sheriff spent several minutes speaking to the people but he saw that it seemed a wasted effort, and he soon returned to the porch of the embattled structure. Whitlock once more began to shout from the porch of the jail, and as he did so, a figure began to make its way through the milling, shouting people to the porch of the jail. He stepped onto the porch and many people recognized the person to be Reverend Geiser of the First Cumberland Presbyterian Church. There was a brief hush in the forefront of the mob as the minister raised his arms and called out to them. For a few short moments they studied this new addition to their opposition, then in a voice, they hooted and shouted the man to silence. As Whitlock and Geiser exchanged looks, a number of stones hit the jail. The minister would be remembered as the only man in the city, besides the Sheriff, who had tried to reason with the mob at the county jail.

Whitlock now went back inside the jail and removed a twelve gauge Winchester riot gun from its rack in his office. He filled his coat pocket with number four buckshot shells and told his men that if it came to shooting, all they needed to do was to keep him supplied with ammunition. As he spoke to the deputies, they heard the sound of shattering glass as rocks were thrown through the windows of the jail. Whitlock now went upstairs to his wife and told her to keep the children on the floor and away from the windows.

While the Sheriff was speaking to his family, the last of the streetlights was shattered with a well aimed stone. Now the area was illuminated only by distant street lamps and the brightly lit porch of the jail. A few torches and lanterns were carried by members of the mob, but these cast only small circles of soft light on those near to them. Winfield Baker was satisfied with the work on the streetlights, now he walked to the jail and went to the front door.

Deputy Newlin heard a loud knock on the door, and he looked out a peep hole to see who was there. He saw the Kentuckian hammering the door with his fist. Newlin asked him what he wanted and Baker told him, as he had told VanVickle earlier, that he wanted the keys to the jail. The deputy informed the rioter the keys would not be turned over. On hearing this, Baker angrily left the porch and walked to the front of the mob, which was now much closer to the jail. He then pulled one of the revolvers from his belt and turned and fired the first shot of the night at the brick building. Now rocks, bricks, and other missiles were hurled at the jail in a barrage as the mob was further infuriated at the Sheriff's decision not to turn over the prisoners.

Inside the jail Whitlock was scribbling out his second telegram to be sent to the state capitol. Its message would further increase the feeling of helplessness already gripping Roy Reece;

Governor Richard Yates
Mob stormed jail / One man burned alive / probably two or three killed / Can't you order Battery A / Do not send Negro Company
H.H. Whitlock, Sheriff

As soon as a deputy left with the wire the Sheriff once again returned to the porch of the jail. This time he held the shotgun cradled in his arms as he walked to the low railing that ran around the edge of the wide verandah. The porch floor was now covered with all matter of debris that had been thrown by the rioters. Whitlock eyed those in front of him silently as they continued to scream at the top of their lungs, "Lynch! Lynch! Lynch!"

Chapter Nine

An attorney and a businessman had been drinking in the bar of the Aetna Hotel and they decided to walk down to the jail to observe the excitement. As the two made their way down Vermilion Street, they were amazed at the large number of people who were attempting to reach the embattled jail. They were surprised to see many women and young boys in the crush of people. They judged the boys to be in their early teens but some of them were much younger. The sound of the mob was articulated into a roar that rolled up the street to meet them. "Lynch! Lynch! Lynch!" was exploding from hundreds of throats as the mob pressed forward. A cheer would break out as the chant was completed. Horses were running loose. Buggies and rigs were left unattended, their steeds still attached, where their excited drivers and passengers had left them.

The men could see a lone figure on the brightly lit porch of the jail facing the mob. When they drew nearer, they recognized the figure as Hardy Whitlock. He held a shotgun in his hands. They walked on to the corner of South and Vermilion Streets where the body of Metcalf was still smoldering on a bed of coals. They stood and observed the rioting a few minutes before starting back north on Vermilion. They both agreed it was only a matter of time until the jail was overrun and more bodies would join the one on the fire.

The two decided to stop at Shaffer's Saloon for a drink at 13 South Vermilion. When they entered the establishment, they found it unattended and men were running in and helping themselves to the liquor stock and then running back to the action on the street.

Whitlock stopped trying to reason with those facing him. When he became silent, a member of the mob stepped onto the lower steps of the porch. The Sheriff slowly walked to meet the man, who was

Winfield Baker. As he did, a few of his deputies stepped onto the porch behind the lawman.

Baker held a revolver in each hand. Now he spoke in a loud voice, addressing the Sheriff, but his words carried to the lawless horde that stood behind him. He told Whitlock the mob would either enter the jail or destroy it. He further informed the lawman he was a bad individual and was no stranger to jails.

Whitlock told Baker no one would be admitted to the jail and no prisoners would be turned over. He further informed him the man they most wanted, James Wilson, had not been found guilty of any crime nor had he been identified by the victim. He then told Baker and those standing near that he would use the shotgun to defend the jail if they made an attempt to enter the structure. This brought on a loud shout from those nearest the confrontation. A number of men taunted the Sheriff to shoot. Baker turned and left the Sheriff, and Whitlock and his deputies returned to the inside of the jail building.

Once more the men in the jail heard a loud knock on the door, and when a deputy looked out, he saw a Western Union runner with a telegram in his hand. The messenger was admitted, and the Sheriff read the first telegram he received from the capitol. It informed him Governor Yates was on vacation and Lieutenant Governor Northcott was now acting governor. The message did not inform the Sheriff that Northcott was also out of reach. Now Whitlock scribbled his third and final telegram to the state capitol.

Acting Governor W.A. Northcott-Spfled. Ills.
hurry militia if possible / terrible condition affairs /
unable to Cope with situation
H.H. Whitlock, Sheriff

Whitlock would have to cope, for there would be no help from Springfield or any other quarter. The thousands of rioters and those who were observing them from a safe distance knew they were approaching a climax to the confrontation at the jail. The rioters had worked themselves up to a feverish pitch of excitement, and whiskey bottles were being passed freely from hand to hand. Many of the participants were now so drunk they did not realize the dangerous situation they were a part of.

Bessie Dodge now took an active part in the rioting. She climbed into the box of a wagon that was parked across the street from the county jail. Then the red haired woman gathered her long skirts into her hand and climbed onto the spring seat of the vehicle. She now had a commanding view of the jail and the mob gathered around it. Her voice rose like a siren as she implored the rioters to attack the jail. Heads turned to see where this new sound of encouragement was coming from. When the men saw Dodge standing on the wagon, they seemed to surge forward in response.

On the south side of the jail, a large group of men had picked up a railroad tie. They were moving determinedly toward the door of the jail. Before they reached it, Whitlock stepped out the door and addressed the men holding the battering ram. He urged them to put down the tie and to return to their homes. He told them the law would take care of those who were prisoners in the jail. The Sheriff made three different impassioned pleas to the men on the downside of the jail. Once they were moved into putting the battering ram down, but they just as quickly picked it back up.

Then Whitlock once again entered the jail. He had made his last appeal. He could see words were not going to have any affect on those who were now determined to storm the building. On the outside he could hear the roar of the mob punctuated by an occasional shot that sent a bullet thudding into the jail. He had seen men brutally mutilating the corpse that was still smoldering on the street corner. The fingers, toes, and ears of the lynching victim had been severed by sharp knives as ghoulish souvenir hunters were on the scene. It was decision time for the lawman. His mind had long been made up as to what he would do if he were ever faced with this situation.

It was apparent to everyone that the rioters were totally out of control, though Winfield Baker and a few others had assumed leadership roles. It was also apparent there was not going to be any move by the elected leaders of the city of Danville, or its prominent citizens, to stop the lawless horde until it had stormed the jail. It all came down on the shoulders of the former farm boy from the small community of Georgetown, Illinois.

On the south side of the jail, Adam Murray was shouting encouragement to the men with the heavy railroad tie. The miner had a vantage point on a fence post and his voice was heard above the roar of the mob. When the men holding the tie looked at Murray, he fired a shot at the jail with his revolver and waved them forward.

Isaac Slade had been involved in the night's violence from the beginning. He had watched the lynching victim, Metcalf, spin in the air as the bullets struck him while he was hanging on East Main Street. He had helped drag the battered body to it's present location at the corner of South and Vermilion. Slade was now moving among the huge crowd, warning the women and youngsters to move back. He informed them the jail was going to be dynamited.

The men holding the tie surged forward and swung the heavy timber against the door of the jail. A triumphant shout went up from the mob as the attack finally began. Again and again the tie crashed into the door as the men were encouraged by the loud roar behind them. A number of shots were now echoing to the river bottom and up and down the streets as the armed members of the mob began to fire at the jail in earnest.

The bottom panel on the door gave way and the tie came plunging into the jail. Deputy Newlin had been standing near the door. When the panel shattered, he drew his revolver and stepped to the opening. The men holding the battering ram were surprised to see the deputy open the damaged door and point a pistol in their direction. When Newlin fired over the heads of the rioters, they threw down the tie and ran toward the rear of the mob.

Whitlock was at the front door of the jail when he heard the loud explosion from his deputy's weapon. He now went to the scene of the shooting and once again told Newlin and the others not to shoot unless ordered to do so. At this point Laura Whitlock came down the stairs and asked the Sheriff for a weapon, but once again her husband asked her to remain upstairs and look after the children.

The mob was becoming more and more racially motivated. The cries were now directed at the Sheriff, and he was cautioned against shooting at white men to protect the black prisoners.

The effect of Newlin's shot soon wore off and once again the mob began to press forward. Now Whitlock stepped to the porch of the jail and fired two shots from his shotgun over the heads of the rioters. Suddenly, the individuals in the mob realized that someone, other than the prisoners and the lawmen, might be injured. Some of the rioters backed up from the jail. The onlookers who had been at a safe distance moved even farther from the man with the riot gun.

Whitlock stepped back inside his jail and watched the mob

through a peephole. For a few brief moments it seemed the rioters might lose their nerve. Then from her perch on the wagon, Bessie Dodge's voice rose in the humid air.

"Lynch the Sheriff, he's no better than the niggers!" rang out as the red haired harlot waved the men forward.

The mob seemed to gain new vigor from Dodge's voice, and it was soon joined by hundreds of others. They had seen the lawman shoot, but he had shot over their heads. A large number of those pressing forward were fueled by liquor from Donnelly's, Foher's, Miller's, Shermayer's, and scores of other saloons in the downtown area. Justice in the United States had long been associated with a short rope and a long drop without the necessity of a trial and due process. Now the mob was ready to carry out their version of vigilante justice. The rioters were now marching to a new battle cry. "Lynch the Sheriff! Lynch the Sheriff!"

Years later, Judge Morton Thompson, would comment that Sheriff Whitlock was a rare commodity in an era when corrupt politicians and political hacks were the rule. The mob assaulting the county jail in Danville was under the impression it was facing a political sheriff, when in reality, Whitlock was a law and order man. Thompson would comment later, "Hardy didn't give a damn about the odds, he was hell bent to uphold the law."

Now the historic moment was at hand. No sheriff in the United States had ever successfully defended his jail from a mob like this. The rioters had already tasted blood and were driven by the desire to spill more. If they weren't stopped, they would leave a dark spot on the image of the city of Danville that would not be easily erased. It was now the twentieth century and these nineteenth century men were going to be introduced to a new day.

Sheriff Whitlock was done with trying to reason with the rioters. He was finished with his warning shots. As he looked out his peephole, he could see the women and small boys had retreated a far distance from the jail. Evidently, the warning shots had caused this. On the street corner he could still see a small fire flickering around the body of Metcalf. People were shoving at each other in their haste to see the charred remains. In front of the jail he saw Winfield Baker near the jail, encouraging the others to move forward.

When he moved to the south side of the jail, he saw Murray still calling for the men there to storm the door. As Murray called out, the men began to move forward and they now held a heavy iron railroad rail in their hands. Nearly fifty men were gripping the new battering ram that had replaced the tie. In the distance the lawman could see a number of horse drawn ambulances drive up, their attendants standing by.

Whitlock now called Deputy Newlin to his side. "There is only one way to handle a man like that," the Sheriff said, indicating Murray, "and that is to kill him." He then told his deputy that he was going to open the south door of the jail and shoot at the miner with his shotgun. At the same time he ordered Newlin to shoot Murray with his revolver. The Sheriff then said he didn't want anyone to know the younger lawman was involved in the shooting, that he himself would take the responsibility. He did not want his deputies to be endangered in the future by the actions about to take place.

The men on the south lawn of the jail were surprised when the door opened and Sheriff Whitlock sprang out. Once again he raised the barrel of his Winchester but this time as the stock of the gun came firmly against his shoulder he did not aim over the heads of the mob. The sights fell on the man who was shouting instructions to the rioters. With an explosion that filled the night, Adam Murray was felled.

Murry dropped to the ground, crying, "My God, I've been shot!"

Looks of surprise, anger, and uncertainty appeared on the faces of those facing the jail as Murray fell. The men holding the iron railroad rail stared at the Sheriff as the Winchester swung in their direction. They were still holding on when the first shot of buckshot ripped down the rail, tearing off fingers, and punching holes in bodies. They dropped the rail with screams of pain when the next shot from Whitlock's riot gun laid a number of the jails attackers on the ground. Some of the men crawled or were carried away by their accomplices, others lay still, waiting on the ambulances to pick them up.

The mob retreated, injuring a number of people in the wild rush away from the Sheriff and his riot gun. The area around the jail was clear as the Sheriff shut the damaged door and barred it on the inside. He began gathering his deputies to go outside and clear the area. No one had been wounded on the inside of the jail by the gunfire or rocks that had come through the windows.

The shooting from the rioters had stopped when the lawmen fired their guns at Murray. For a few brief minutes it seemed the trouble was over. Then from the outside the voice of Bessie Dodge once more could be heard imploring the rioters to renew the attack. Winfield Baker was also waving the men forward with his revolver, but the Kentuckian himself remained a safe distance from the jail. The thousands of onlookers, now well back from the building under attack, also added their voices calling for another assault. The rioters in the front line responded and once again began to move toward the jail.

Before Whitlock and his men were able to exploit the brief advantage the first shots had gained for them, the attack was renewed. This time the rail had been carried to the front of the jail and men were crowding forward to help swing it against the door. Andrew Swafford, a veteran of the Civil War, was badly injured as he was crushed between the rail and the door of the jail.

Bessie Dodge was crying out. "He shot white men to protect the niggers, hang the Sheriff!"

The street was soon filled with the mob rushing forward to attack the jail. Once more a few shots rang out and thudded into the bricks of the Vermilion County jail. Jack Walton was so intoxicated he could hardly stand up, but he was waving the men forward like a wobbly general on a brick paved battle field. "Lynch the niggers! Lynch the niggers!" was the new cry coming from thousands of throats, now hoarse from a night of shouting.

Then the front door of the jail was jerked open, and the men were face to face with the Sheriff and his shotgun, some of them only a few feet from the end of his gun barrel. Whitlock's coat was soaked through with sweat and his hat was pushed back slightly on his head. As his big hands brought the Winchester up, those in the front tried to move back, but they were held in place by those behind them. Those who could see the lawman's eyes had no doubt as to what was going to happen next. Winfield Baker moved to the rear of the mob, Bessie Dodge fell silent. Isaac Slade was trapped in the front. He would relate later that the look on Whitlock's face, "scared the hell out of us." Then in seconds it was over.

Whitlock once again fired down the iron rail and men fell on both sides of the battering ram as the rail clattered to the ground. When the mob did not break up, the lawman continued to pump buckshot into them, walking forward as he fired, then reloading and firing again. He did not stop until the rioters were in full retreat. Left behind were a number of men who were unable to run. They cried out in pain as they waited for ambulances to make their way through the panicked rioters.

Bessie Dodge once more shouted for the people to attack the Sheriff, but this time her call was ignored. When she noticed the street was quickly becoming empty, she began to climb down from the wagon, her voice was nearly gone from all the screaming. Jack Walton was still staggering in the street and shouting for a new attack, but he too was ignored by the men running from the scene. The sight of their comrades falling to the ground streaming blood had sobered up many of those who were intoxicated. Some of the men seemed surprised by their wounds and stared dumbly back at the Sheriff with looks of disbelief as they lay on the ground.

Whitlock and his deputies were quick to exploit the situation as they filed out on the porch and shouted for the few who remained near the jail to leave. One man turned and cried out that they were only trying to carry out the law. Whitlock's voice boomed out his reply "Here stands the law and it will not break nor will it bend." This time the lawmen were obeyed as they gave the order to clear the street.

A few of the men would remain across the street from the jail until nearly daybreak, but they offered no further violence. They only made a few catcalls to the armed deputies who spent the night patrolling the porch and grounds of the jail.

The ambulances quickly picked up the wounded men from the street and took them to the hospitals. Some would be treated and released, others would remain. Many of the wounded were taken home by friends and family. A number of injured were laid out in a nearby barn to await treatment.

Metcalf's remains were picked up about three in the morning by Turner, Learnard & Son, Undertakers. The body would be placed on public display the next day.

A wire came in during the night from the state capitol informing the Sheriff that troops would be sent and should be in the city before noon of the 26th. Roy Reece had finally located one of those in authority and had obtained legal release of the militia.

As the rioters left the scene of the night's violence, they once again became individuals, no longer were they part of a lawless army. One graying veteran of the War Between the States, who was limping away from the scene, was asked by a reporter what had happened.

"Why hell," the man replied in a still surprised voice. "Old Hardy shot me."

The rioters thought the trouble was over as they left the jail. They would have agreed with one attorney's view of the night's bedlam when he commented "the boys were a little mischievous."

But the man wearing the star who stood on the porch of his jail would have a different idea. Through the night he had heard the mob cry out that they were trying to bring justice to the people. In the coming weeks Whitlock would see that they did see justice. The event was far from over as the street cleared and people returned to their homes.

Part 2

Arrest and Indictments

Chapter Ten

The robins sang their first notes of the day as the hint of dawn tinted the eastern sky on the morning of July 26, 1903. The summer heat wave continued to grip Vermilion County as the first citizens began to stir on the streets of Danville.

Early risers were greeted with a sight that was unusual for a Sunday morning in the county seat. They found a number of heavily armed city policemen standing along Vermilion Street in the block between the courthouse and the county jail. The men were red-eyed from lack of sleep and their stance showed they were weary from the long night's vigil. The officers had not helped in the defense of the county jail, but they had been on duty to keep looting and destruction of property down as the rioters rampaged through Danville. After Sheriff Whitlock had shattered the mob at the jail with buckshot, the city police had made a sweep in the public square and sent the people still gathered there home. Then they had taken up positions along the street to help control any further outbreak of violence.

With the coming of daylight, Sheriff Whitlock sent his deputies home for rest. One of them lived nearby in a rooming house and would be available if trouble broke out. All of those who had participated in the defense of the jail were exhausted.

Before Whitlock went to his bed for a rest, he surveyed what the rioters had left behind at the county jail. The windows of the building had been shattered by bullets, rocks, and bricks. Two doors had been damaged beyond repair by the battering rams used by the mob. Clubs, pitchforks, bottles, and other trash covered the area where the people had milled about during the rioting. A large number of hats and caps were scattered about where men and boys had lost them in the wild excitement of the previous night. The heavy iron rail used as a battering ram still lay where the rioters had left it on the steps of the jail, it extended across the sidewalk and into the street. It would take a number of men to remove it from the premises. Dark stains marked the trail the wounded rioters had taken in their retreat from the jail.

Whitlock saw a small pile of ashes and an unburned portion of railroad tie at the corner of South and Vermilion Streets. This marked the spot where John Metcalf had been cremated by the mob. Empty brass shell casings glittered in the early morning sun where they had been ejected from the guns of members of the mob. On the east side of Vermilion Street, the wagon Bessie Dodge had shouted from the night before stood like a forgotten monument to the violence.

As the Sheriff climbed the stairs to the second floor of the county jail building, the curious were already beginning to appear on the street. Whitlock ate breakfast with his wife and then laid down for a short rest. The lawman seldom missed a day in church, he was a devout Presbyterian, but this was one Sunday he would be occupied by other matters.

Even before the Sheriff went to his bed for rest there was a new group of sharp-eyed men in the city looking into the previous nights excitement. They were the reporters from the big city papers. They had descended on the city "like a swarm of locusts" one local newsman would report. This was made possible by the twenty-seven passenger trains that made stops in Danville on Sunday. On a weekday there were more than fifty passenger trains pulling into the busy terminals of the city.

The newsmen were joined by a growing number of others as they walked the route the rioters had taken on the previous night. First to be surveyed was the ravaged city hall on Walnut Street, its broken windows staring out blindly at the crowd gathered in front. Then the curious began the trek to Shermayer's Saloon on East Main, talking in hushed voices as they walked in small groups. The route was clearly marked by broken windows in many of the buildings bordering the street.

At Shermayer's the pole where Metcalf was hung seemed to be the center of attraction. A piece of hemp rope that had been left tied to the pole had already been cut away by an enterprising souvenir hunter. Those who had taken part in the previous night's violence were quick to point out the highlights of the tour. In front of Miller's Bakery near the Wabash tracks they called attention to the blood stains that marked the spot where Henry Gatterman had died.

The curious then walked on to the county jail where Sheriff Whitlock had brought the night's violence to an end. They quickly gathered up the spent cartridges from the street, and some removed small pieces of charred wood from the ashes where Metcalf had been cremated. This early morning tour was just the beginning of a day that would see Danville filled with one of the largest crowds ever to occupy the city.

Whitlock had only been resting a short time when he was paid a visit by attorney George T. Buckingham. The lawyer complimented the Sheriff on his handling of the mob the previous night. He also told the lawman he would have the full support of the Vermilion County Bar Association in any actions he wanted to pursue concerning the rioters. Before the attorney left, a deputy came into the jail's austere office and told the Sheriff there were a number of men making threats against his life. Some of those seeking revenge against Whitlock were reportedly friends of Adam Murray. When the deputy and Buckingham left the jail, they were met by a group of reporters searching for the Sheriff.

The journalists had already shown a little disappointment at the lack of physical damage to the city on the Vermilion. The messages they had received by wire during the night had led them to believe they might find a smoking ruin where the city of Danville had once stood. Now as they entered the damaged county jail building and walked into the office where Whitlock sat, they studied the man who had stopped the violence. One reporter would describe him as being a tired looking man with dark circles under his eyes, an individual with little patience for the press.

Whitlock listened to the barrage of questions hurled at him by the newsmen standing in his office. With their stubby pencils ready to write, the journalists knew they were facing the source of a top news story. They had been disappointed at the lack of property destruction they had found in the wake of the riot, now they were going to be more disappointed by the lack of response from the big man in the rumpled suit facing them.

When asked if he knew how many men he had shot, Whitlock

truthfully answered that he did not. Questioned about the possibility of rioters being arrested, the lawman responded there "most likely" would be arrests if he had anything to do with it. When asked questions concerning the threats on his life and why he had shot white men to protect black prisoners, the Sheriff did not respond. When Whitlock quit answering questions, the reporters gradually fell silent until the only sound in the office was the hollow ticking of the clock on the wall. The newsmen then took their leave and left the lawman alone to plan his next move.

While Whitlock was talking to the reporters, Judge Morton Thompson was viewing the scene of the riot. Thompson had been a busy man since returning to Danville from Chicago in the early morning hours. The Judge had already talked to Mayor Beard and State's Attorney Keeslar. He had also had an early meeting with Colonel Buckingham before that worthy called on the Sheriff. Now the Judge, called Mort by his friends, returned to his elm shaded home on Pine Street. He had decided to meet with the Sheriff in the coming week rather than bother the exhausted lawman on this busy day.

Thompson was outraged at what had occurred in the city and he was well aware of what would have happened if the Sheriff had not stopped the riot when he did. On his tour of the city on this early Sunday morning he had not seen one black person on the street. When he had passed through the neighborhood where the majority of the minority population lived, the area had been silent and seemed deserted.

The Judge was of medium height with a husky build. He had dark, piercing eyes and his black hair was showing touches of gray. Though he was nearly fifty years old, Thompson's features gave him a youthful appearance, a bushy mustache added a touch of maturity to his countenance. As he entered his home, his mouth was set in a tight line, and he told his wife Mary that someone must be brought to justice for the violence that had swept through the city.

The deep resonant sound of church bells rang throughout Danville as the faithful were called to worship. As the pews filled in the holy places of the city, the ministers were preparing to raise their voices in protest over the actions of the rioters. While the curious filled the streets, the religious leaders filled their sanctuaries with rage and indignation that such an event as the riot could occur in a civilized society. There was standing room only in many of the churches as worshipers gathered to hear the sermons on the day following the night of madness.

The one man who had tried to help the Sheriff calm the mob at the county jail found his church full on this stifling Sunday morning. While fans fluttered in the congregation, Reverend Geiser of the First Cumberland Presbyterian Church delivered a stirring sermon. He took for his text, "Righteousness Exalteth a Nation, But Sin is a Reproach to Any People."

Reverend Greening of the Lincoln Methodist Church told a full house that he would like to see a mob "get at the root of such evil and smash the saloons which cause such crimes." Pastor Gibbs told his flock at the First M.E. Church there was still "hope, hope that the saloon power will one day fall."

But it was perhaps the sonorous voice of Willis Parsons, minister of the First Presbyterian Church, that touched nearest to the true causes of the crimes. His church stood at the corner of North and Franklin, only a block from the wrecked city hall. The pastor pointed out to the congregation how near they were to the place where lawlessness had reigned less than twenty four hours before. He then told the worshipers who filled the pews of the chapel, "no people can prosper in the truest sense and for any length of time where there are antagonistic interests and race hatred."

While church was in session, the Sheriff had received news troops were arriving at the C&EI Station. Though the need for the militia was not as pressing as it had been a few hours before, the lawman knew the presence of the armed soldiers would help to calm the population in the coming days. Whitlock held no misconceptions about what his actions of the previous night would incur. He knew he had been acting entirely within his rights, but he was aware there would be people who would hate him for the rest of their lives for what he did. The presence of troops might give that hatred a time to cool before it exploded into violence.

At the depot a number of residents had gathered to watch the soldiers disembark from the special train that had delivered them to Danville. The men were from the Seventh Regiment of Chicago and were known as the Irish Seventh. They had been given the name because of the large number of Irish-Americans in the unit. The soldiers were experienced in handling civil disobedience, having seen duty during labor troubles in Mt. Vernon and Chicago. A few of the men were veterans of the Spanish-American War.

Armed soldiers were no strangers to the city, on previous visits they had been called upon because of labor unrest. In 1894 state troops had shot and killed two women in the Grape Creek area during a miners' strike. Following the shootings the miners had stopped all rail traffic through that mining community for more than a week. This was the first time the militia had been called to Danville to protect prisoners in the custody of the law. As the young men stepped smartly off the train, they found a welcoming committee of unfriendly faces.

The soldiers were quickly formed into ranks for the march to the jail and as they did so, they were treated to jeers and catcalls by the locals. The militia wore the new khaki uniforms recently issued by the government and bystanders who asked were informed they each carried forty rounds of ammunition for their rifles.

As the men began to march toward the jail, they were followed by the crowd which was growing in numbers. The four companies of armed militia were not intimidated by the taunts being hurled at them as they moved down the same streets Metcalf's body had passed over the previous night. The rhythmic sound of their quick step march on the brick paved street and the sharp commands of the officers prompted one newsman to write that these were not "tin soldiers."

The militia reached the county jail without incident and a squad was detailed to begin walking guard duty around the building. A loud cheer went up from the prisoners inside the jail when they saw the armed troopers outside. Colonel Clasby, who arrived as commander of the militia, went to meet with Whitlock while his men settled in the market house across the street from the jail.

Whitlock met the army officer on the porch of the jail. The county lawman was standing there watching the growing number of people who had followed the soldiers down the street. The two men shook hands and Clasby commented it looked like the Sheriff had experienced an eventful night. Whitlock was visibly relieved to have the military present but he was regarding the people who were beginning to congregate in front of the jail with a wary eye. As the two men left the porch and walked through the shattered door to the inside of the jail, a squad of soldiers cleared the street. For the first time in nearly twenty-four hours the lawman began to relax.

Colonel Clasby was no stranger at handling civilian problems. He was a ten year veteran of the militia and had been called to duty in a number of labor disputes. The officer was well aware that the way to handle mob problems was to keep the people from congregating. He now proposed to the Sheriff that patrols be extended beyond the area of the jail to the blocks that composed the downtown area.

Before Whitlock would agree to putting armed military patrols out in the city, he had to contact Mayor Beard. The Sheriff knew many residents of the city and county would not approve of armed soldiers walking the streets of Danville.

Beard told Whitlock he had permission to do whatever he felt necessary to insure peace in the city. The Mayor stressed his desire that there be no reoccurrence of events similar to the rioting of the previous night. Beard had already been approached by reporters questioning the actions of the city police during the riot and he had refused to answer their questions. He would do the same to the flood of telegrams being wired to him from all over the nation.

As soon as the area where the troops were to patrol had been worked out between the two men, Clasby left to find personal quarters. It was now growing late in the forenoon and a few of Whitlock's deputies began to return to the jail. They had rested a few hours and were now anxious to find out what the Sheriff planned to do next.

Newlin, Runyan, and others gathered in the small office the Sheriff occupied in the county jail. The men found Whitlock, a man slow to anger, showing the first real signs of rage over the events of the previous night. Their leader then told them he would see the leaders of the mob arrested, prosecuted, and sent to prison if it were his last earthly act. He told the men his wife and children had crouched on the floor of the jail in terror while the rioters had fired shots into the windows of the residential section of the jail. He asked his deputies, who were mildly surprised at his show of anger, what kind of men would shoot at a building where children lived. He then told those gathered around he had already been approached by an individual who had asked that the riot be forgotten. He also told the men about his visit from Colonel Buckingham and that he had the support of Judge Thompson and Prosecutor Keeslar. Deputy Newlin told the Sheriff he would be "more than glad" to let some of the rioters see the inside of the jail cells since they had been so set on getting into them on the previous night. When the meeting broke up the deputies had a list of people they were to arrest. Some were names, others were only descriptions; the names would come later.

By one o'clock the city of Danville was full of people. Every train that arrived was filled with those who had heard about the trouble on the previous night. The dismissal of church had also added large numbers of the curious who had not been able to view the scene of the riot during the morning.

On North Vermilion Street, the firm of Turner, Learnard & Son had placed the remains of Metcalf on public display. People quickly lined up for a block to see the grisly remains of the construction worker. Before the afternoon was over the line would extend for several blocks as people sweltered in the July sun. At the funeral parlor of Harry Waltz, where the body of Henry Gatterman had been taken, a large crowd also gathered.

The militia was now walking the downtown area of Danville in two man patrols, but the people did not seem to be in a troublesome mood. The only act of violence occurred when Ed Liggett attacked a private standing guard in front of the jail. The soldier quickly overpowered the man and he was taken before Justice of the Peace Grant by two of the Sheriff's deputies. Grant fined Liggett $100 and the offender was reportedly greatly subdued by the fine and his arrest.

By the middle of the afternoon a light breeze was stirring the humid air and tugging at the hats of the people crowding the streets. The Governor's personal secretary, Colonel Ogelsby, now arrived on the scene and went directly from the depot to the jail to confer with Whitlock. The Sheriff informed the chief executive's representative that things were well in hand and the people were cooperating with the law. Ogelsby then went to the Western Union office and sent a wire to the Governor of Illinois expressing his view that the people were in a restless mood. This was the beginning of a rift between Whitlock and the Governor that would explode into a public exchange of words in a few weeks.

As dusk began to gather in the city on the Vermilion there were rumors out that some of the rioters might be arrested. It was also rumored the Mayor had stated there were a hundred good people in the mob, though this statement was never substantiated by Danville's leader. The Sheriff had been told by a number of people he had used poor judgment when he shot white men to "protect the blacks." Whitlock never wavered from his position that he had been elected to uphold the law. He left no doubt in the minds of those who tried to persuade him to forget the riot that he would proceed with arrests.

The crowds on the streets of Danville thinned as the sun disappeared on the western horizon. The rural people had left the brick paved streets of the city to take the dirt roads that led to their country homes. The children who rode home with their parents in the quiet of the evening would remember the riot of the previous day for the rest of their lives. Over eighty years later Webber Graves would remember Hardy Whitlock being pointed out to him when he was a child, as the lawmen who had shot "all those men" when they attacked his jail.

In the saloons on this night after the riot, the participants were regaling others with stories of their part in the violence of the previous night. It was noted by the saloon keepers, as they served up drinks and polished their bars, that many who had been nowhere near the riot were anxious to have others believe they had participated in it. In a few days there would not be a person in the county who would admit he had taken an active part in the violence of July 25, 1903.

Chapter Eleven

Danville was quieter on the morning of July 27th. Whitlock held an early morning meeting with Colonel Clasby and found there had been no trouble during the previous night. A number of reporters were at the county jail to interview the Sheriff, but he declined to comment on the riot or what he planned to do about those involved in it.

The reporters did not let the Sheriff's lack of cooperation keep them from writing some sensational stories about the events taking place in Danville. They referred to Danville as a strife torn city and continued to call the lynching and riot a race war. One reporter wrote the troops sent to Danville were trampled by a mob. While many of the newsmen gave the happenings in Danville honest coverage, others reported events in a manner that conveyed little of the truth.

Rumors abounded in the city of arrests that were going to be made, but the rioters did not believe there would be any further actions taken. Many of them felt because there had been thousands of people on the streets on Saturday, it would be impossible for the law to prosecute individuals. It was also rumored no justice of the peace would sign arrest warrants.

The Vermilion County Bar Association met and gave Whitlock a vote of approval on the way he had handled the mob. They also endorsed the idea of prosecuting the offenders to the full extent of the law. There was also a message of encouragement from U. S. Representative Joseph G. Cannon, and a warning that lawlessness in Danville must be stopped. The view was not shared by all the residents of the county. As businessmen gathered to dine on their fifteen cent roast beef and drink their five cent coffee for lunch, there were many who believed the matter of the riot should be dropped. They felt there was no need for the Sheriff to make arrests.

The railroad post office cars that came through the city carried messages swiftly to friends and relatives of Danville residents beyond the border of Illinois. The postal clerks, who picked up the mail at the various towns and sorted it along the way, carried a postcard from a Danville resident to a friend in Florida. The message stated "there was a riot here Saturday night, Negro lynched, now a big howl about nothing, some may be arrested."

In the saloons, gamblers were betting the Sheriff would not live long enough to bring anyone to trial. There had been numerous threats made against the lawman by friends and relatives of those shot at the jail. There was also talk of storming the jail again, but this threat would not be taken seriously as long as there were armed soldiers in the city.

The undertakers at Turner, Learnard & Son waited until mid-morning for some family member or friend to claim the body of the lynching victim. When no one came forward to arrange for the burial of Metcalf, it was decided to place him in the Potter's field section of Spring Hill Cemetery. The construction worker was placed in lot forty-four, row one, of the burial ground. There was no one present at the burial, other than the workers, and no service was held. No one ever inquired about the man following his lynching, though rumors persisted that he had a wife and she had fled the city.

The soldiers patrolling the streets of Danville continued to be heckled by residents, but they were less of a novelty on their second day in Danville. The area where they were quartered had been dubbed Camp Whitlock by the locals. The troops were the first thing the prisoners in the jail looked for when morning came. The militia did not stop people from walking in the area of the jail, but they did make them keep moving and did not allow them to gather in groups.

The hospitals in the city had a number of gunshot patients from the night of the riot. An even larger number of the wounded had been treated and dismissed. Conservative figures put the number of men who had been shot at about two dozen, others thought as many as forty were wounded on the night of the lynching.

Whitlock spent the day preparing arrest warrants, and his deputies quietly began gathering information on those involved in the riot. By evening of the 27th the names and descriptions of many of the riot leaders were beginning to come together.

Chapter Twelve

July 28th was the day of burial for Henry Gatterman, the man killed by John Metcalf. The funeral was held at Grace Methodist Church and the small chapel was filled to overflowing for the service. Many of those in attendance stood on the sidewalk and street in front of the church.

The Reverend A. M. Wells told those gathered in the church, "The dreadful circumstances surrounding the death of this man suggests the fact that there are three great evils existing in our land that need mastering by a strong hand or they will one day crush us as a people into dust. First is intemperance. The start of all the trouble was the fact that the Negro had been drinking. The mob at the jail was for the most part made up of young men who spend their time about saloons. Second is race hatred. It was not because of the awfulness of his crime the colored man was lynched, it was because his skin was black. There is no race war in Danville, but the facts exist that there is a strong hatred between the races. Third is mob law."

Gatterman was an Army veteran and Battery A, Danville's home unit, provided an honor guard for the funeral. The funeral procession that slowly moved from the church to Spring Hill Cemetery was one of the largest in the city's history. Many businesses had closed down for the funeral and people stood on the sidewalks and watched the cortege pass by, a number of children were waving small American flags.

When the procession made the turn from Main to Hazel Street, a contingent of eighteen soldiers of the occupying militia were marching toward the mourners from the north. The men of the Seventh stepped to the curb and came to attention as the horse drawn hearse approached. As the flower covered coffin passed, the soldiers removed their headgear in a show of respect. The men continued to stand at attention until the last of the mourners had passed them by. The actions of the militia were viewed favorably by the public and would improve residents' acceptance of their presence in the city.

Justice of the Peace Payton informed the Sheriff he would not sign arrest warrants for any person accused of taking part in the lynching or the riot. The statement by the magistrate reflected the feelings of many residents of the county. While there was a large public clamor for those involved in the riot to be brought to justice, there was an opposing undercurrent of feeling that whispered for the matter to be dropped.

Laura Whitlock was encouraged by her father and husband to take the children and leave the city until things quieted down, but she steadfastly refused. She was well aware of the threats being made against her husband, but the small woman was strong willed, and she would not consent to move from her home in the jail.

Those who had participated in the riot continued to tell of their exploits. Ol Manifield was a farmhand who resided near the small village of Rossville, a dozen miles north of Danville. The farm worker was making no secret of the fact that he had been involved in the lawlessness that shook the county seat. Isaac Slade was displaying the wounds he had received at the jail and giving a full account of the riot to those who gathered to hear his story. The miner would still be displaying his crippled hand and recounting the story decades later to miners of the county.

Word that Justice Payton would not sign any arrest warrants spread rapidly through the city, and many residents believed there would be no arrests. Those who had been apprehensive about their part in the violence breathed a little easier as another day ended with no action by the Sheriff.

July 29th brought cooler weather to Vermilion County. Those in authority hoped it would also cool the anger many people were feeling over the Sheriff's actions at the jail. It was felt all those shot by the law at the jail would survive, though many would be crippled for life as a result of their attack upon the structure.

In the early morning hours a meeting was held in Sheriff Whitlock's office. Present at the meeting were Judge Morton

Thompson, State's Attorney John Keeslar, attorney George T. Buckingham, and Sheriff Whitlock. The meeting sealed the fate of those who had led the attack on the county jail.

While a light breeze gently stirred the leaves of the maple that stood in front of the jail building, the wind of change stirred in the Sheriff's office. Not one of the men present at the meeting ever considered letting the rioters go unpunished. Whitlock, Thompson and Keeslar were sworn to see that justice was done to the best of their abilities and that was what they intended to do. Buckingham would serve as an advisor to the Sheriff and Keeslar in the events that were to come. He was also an acquaintance of Governor Yates and would serve as the Governor's local contact.

Whitlock explained to the others he would be unable to arrest anyone for the murder of Metcalf because he had left the city building before the lynching took place. He pointed out the construction worker had been killed before his remains were butchered and burned in front of his jail. He speculated it would be possible to make arrests after the inquest into the lynching was completed. The Sheriff felt the names of those involved in the killing would come out at the hearing.

It was decided at the meeting to keep at least one company, and possibly two, of the occupying militia in the city for an indefinite period. Two companies had already returned to Camp Lincoln at Springfield. Whitlock thought he could keep order, but it was agreed by the four the presence of troops would have a calming effect on the people during the events yet to come. There had also been rumors circulating there would be an attempt to dynamite the jail. It was felt the military sentries and patrols would reduce the access intruders would have to the building.

Whitlock informed the others there were many citizens who did not feel arrests should be made. He felt when he did make arrests there was a very real danger friends and relatives of those arrested might make an attempt to release them. The Sheriff pointed out if there were arrests made for the murder of Metcalf, those charged would possibly hang. The prospect of white men hanging for the lynching of a black man would almost certainly incite violence.

Judge Thompson told the others the law was to be enforced ,and those who broke it were to be punished. Citizens had broken dozens of laws on the night of July 25th. They had not only broken the law, they had also performed like barbarians from another age. In a civilized society the total disregard for the law could not be permitted. The Judge told the others the guilty must be punished.

The plan agreed on at the meeting was simple; arrest the mob leaders, indict them, immediately summon a petit jury and place them on trial. The meeting broke up before noon, and a wire was sent to the governor informing him the troops would be needed for an indefinite period.

While the Sheriff was holding his meeting in Danville, a reporter from the *Danville Democrat* was making his way to the small village of Alvin to interview the woman allegedly attacked by James Wilson. Though the papers had ran a number of sensational stories concerning the attack that had occurred in the town, as yet no one had interviewed the principals. As the reporter made his way through the pastoral farmland of the county, his counterparts from the large metropolitan cities were continuing to send in their sensational stories from the city on the Vermilion. Readers in Chicago were being told that the militia was being stoned by the residents of Danville. They read one report stating there were two hundred Alvin women in the mob that attacked the jail in the county seat. When one of the reporters was asked why he sent out such stories when he knew they were totally false, he responded his instructions were to "color his reports to the highest point."

The old roll top desk in the Sheriff's office was covered with telegrams delivered by Western Union runners. A few of them were from papers in other cities that did not have their own reporters in Danville, but most of the messages were from people congratulating the Sheriff on his courageous actions at the jail. It was a clear indication public opinion was changing in a nation that had long took little notice of lynch rope justice. As recently as 1900 the Census Bureau had recorded one hundred fifteen lynchings. The true number would have been much higher because many such acts were never recorded. This was especially true when the victim was a member of a minority group.

When the *Democrat* reporter arrived at the small frame home of the Burgess family, he found Mary Burgess was unwilling to talk with him unless her husband was present. Tom Burgess was found and the newsman interviewed the two of them. He was told the woman had been knocked down by the intruder, but she had not been raped. Burgess told the reporter she felt the man might have hurt her badly had she not screamed for help and frightened him. She and her husband both empathized the fact they did not want mob law to rule in the incident. Tom Burgess stated, "There is no use of them (the mob) taking the law into their own hands. We have laws that are sufficient and they should be enforced and I am confident they will be. There is absolutely no excuse for the lawlessness which has been going on in Danville. Again, I say the Sheriff did right in protecting the man (James Wilson) and I sincerely hope no further effort will be made to take him out of the jail." When the interview was printed in the *Democrat,* it put to rest the stories of mobs being organized in the Alvin area.

Danville business and civic leaders were concerned with the way the news was being reported in the large metropolitan papers. They blamed the first target available, the local newsmen. The hometown reporters were not slow in pointing their fingers at the big city journalists who were sending their own news reports over the wires to their editors. When all the dust had cleared over the sensational items that were appearing in the news, it was clear the facts had been distorted. This had occurred both at home and in other cities, but the large metropolitan papers had abused the facts to the greatest degree.

Shortly after noon, Sheriff Whitlock was visited by a group of men who let him know they were concerned about the consequences of making arrests. The lawman listened as it was suggested he make a few token arrests and then turn the men loose after a night or so in jail. He was told it would be extremely unpopular to arrest any of those involved and to hold them for trial. When the self-appointed committee had finished advising, Whitlock, the lawman, dismissed them with a few terse words. He told them he would enforce the law and that meant punishing those who broke it. The Sheriff pointed out it was not a matter of race, it was a matter of law. He stated he had not been shooting white men to protect black men, he had been shooting lawbreakers who were intent on murder. The leader of the group then told the Sheriff if he knew what was best for him, he would go slow in any actions concerning the rioters. The lawman did not agree with this advice either. His course was already set and the wheels of justice were not turning slowly, they were spinning.

Chapter Thirteen

Justice Payton was true to his word. When he was asked to sign arrest warrants for the rioters, he absolutely refused to put his signature on any of the legal documents. But Justices Grant, Hall, Vance, and Patterson did not hesitate to validate the papers. Sheriff Whitlock was working on a score of warrants, and as they were signed, his deputies lost no time in taking action.

Five of the men whose names appeared on the warrants were easy to find, they were still recovering from their wounds in the hospital. Clement Mobaker, Edward Hart, Adam Murray, Harry Devore, and Harry Bicknell were well marked by the buckshot from the Sheriff's riot gun. The five were served with papers as they were recuperating in their hospital beds. They would be taken to the county jail as soon as they were physically able to be moved. Others pulled in by the deputies were Richard Roberts, Isaac Newton Slade, Horace Murphy, Harry Van Gundy, John (Jack) Walton, William Pettis, Cicero Davis, Harry Rennick, and Sherman Cundiff. When arrested, Harry Rennick was wearing only one shoe. His other foot was swathed in bandages, it had been wounded by Whitlock's shotgun blast.

Of those arrested only Cundiff, Van Gundy, and Hart were able to put up the five hundred dollar bond that would keep them out of jail, Harry Rennick would be bailed out later. The men were told Judge Thompson had ordered the present May term of the grand jury to reconvene on August 3rd for the purpose of considering and investigating the riot of July 25th. The accused men were quiet as they took up residence in the building they were accused of storming. There no longer appeared to be safety in numbers. Now it was a question of what the indictments would charge them with, rioting or murder.

On the evening of July 29th a coroner's inquest was held to determine the cause of Henry Gatterman's death. Testifying were Harley Croucher, Charles Shermayer, and Ed Bennett. Soldiers continued to walk their patrols in the downtown area as the coroner's jury listened to the testimony of the witnesses in the courthouse on Danville's square. After all the testimony had been heard, it was determined by the jury that, "Henry Gatterman came to his death by a shot from a pistol in the hands of John D. Metcalf on the evening of July 25th." The jury further found that, "John D. Metcalf was the unlawful slayer of Henry Gatterman."

July 30th promised to be a rewarding one for Sheriff Whitlock and his deputies. The lawmen had been searching for Winfield Baker since the riot. It was feared he had left the area when it became known arrests would be made. But a tipster informed the Sheriff in the early morning hours Baker was back at work on the farm.

Deputies Runyan and Newlin were dispatched by the Sheriff to see if the report was true. Both men were surprised when they saw the Kentuckian mending a fence near the Woodbury farm a short distance northwest of the city. The lawmen covered Baker with their revolvers and searched him. He was carrying a small revolver, but he offered no resistance when the two men approached him. Baker was loaded into their buggy by the deputies for the ride back to the county jail.

Deputy Sheriff Allison was in Rossville, Illinois on this sunny July morning. The Sheriff had sent the deputy there to check with the town marshal on reports stating one of those involved in the riot lived in that city. Allison soon had the name of Ol Manifield and went in search of the individual. He found Manifield doing chores on a farm near the small village. He placed him under arrest and began the long journey back to Danville with Manifield proclaiming his innocence every dusty mile of the way.

John Crist was arrested in Danville and charged with "defacing a public building." One of the deputies translated the charge for Crist, who was not in the least happy at being apprehended. The deputy told the resident, who lived at the corner of North and Gobin Streets, the charges were for throwing rocks at the jail. Crist had no bond money and was locked up with the growing number of accused rioters in the county jail.

Justice Payton was the subject of a meeting between the other justices and State's Attorney Keeslar. Keeslar was informed by the other justices they wanted Payton to do his job or lose his commission. Payton had loudly proclaimed he would not sign any arrest warrants for those involved in the lynching or the rioting. The other justices wanted to present a united front to the residents of the county. They were unwilling to let Payton become a hero, of sorts, because of his stand. Keeslar sent a message to the reluctant Payton explaining if he did not take part in the warrant signing, he would be reported to the governor and would almost certainly have his commission revoked. The slender state's attorney then sent word to Whitlock he should present Payton with an arrest warrant. Whitlock had an unsigned warrant for John Isom, and he lost no time in taking it before Payton. The justice silently signed the warrant for the Hungry Hollow resident and his protest came to an abrupt end. The Sheriff took the signed warrant and personally arrested Isom.

On the evening of the 30th, a coroner's inquest was held to determine the cause of the death of John Metcalf. It was thought the names of those involved in the lynching of the man would be revealed at the hearing. First to testify were officers Leverenz and Foehrer. The two men told of their part in the arrest of Metcalf, but informed the jury they could name no one who had been involved in the actual lynching of the man. Captain Phillips then took the witness chair and gave a brief account of bringing Metcalf to the jail in the paddy wagon. The captain said he was in the jail during the time it was stormed and the prisoner taken from his custody, but he was unable to identify any of those who had broken into the building. The officer related to those listening intently to his testimony, that he had not seen Metcalf after he was taken from the jail.

Officers Poll, Garner, and Liggett were also questioned at length about the attack on the jail and the subsequent lynching, but none of the men could give the identity of those involved in the violence.

Deputy Coroner Henry Hall then questioned a number of men who had been telling marvelous stories about their involvement in the lynching. They had reportedly related how they had climbed the pole and tied the knot in the hangman's rope, how they had struck

Metcalf with clubs as he was dragged away from the jail, and how they had helped cremate the body in front of the county jail. The men now found they could remember none of the stories they had been telling about town. As they took turns being questioned, they reported they knew nothing or very little of the lynching and riot. What information they did have, they reported, came from what they had heard from others and from what they had read in the papers.

It was determined by the coroner's jury that John D. Metcalf had died at the hands of "persons unknown." One of the reporters observing the inquest, sarcastically reported that evidently a "foreign mob" had descended on Danville and wreaked havoc at city hall and then had strangely disappeared. There would be no murder charges filed against those held in custody at the Vermilion County jail.

When the inquest ended, word was passed to the large number of people gathered about the courthouse that it was concluded Metcalf had been killed by unknown assailants. The families and friends of those who had been arrested for their alleged part in the riot were relieved by the verdict of the coroner's jury. There would be no hangings as a result of the lynching.

Chapter Fourteen

As the dog days of August approached Danville, the residents were becoming accustomed to the soldiers patrolling the streets. Resentment of the militia had nearly disappeared after they had paid their respects to the late Henry Gatterman. The officers were now being taken to the Elks Club by local members and the catcalls and heckling of the troops had all but ended. One potentially serious incident had occurred on East Main Street, but it had been handled by the city police. Harry Malone had pulled a large knife on two of the soldiers walking patrol and had attempted to stab the men. Fortunately, officers Foehrer and Leverenz were nearby and were able to arrest Malone before the military men used the rifles they had pointing at their attacker when the police arrived. No one was injured and Malone became a resident of the newly repaired city jail.

The black population was leaving Danville in large numbers. There had been a steady stream of the minority dwellers pouring out of the city since the riot of July 25th. Many of the former Danville residents were reportedly passing through Evansville, Indiana on their way back to their native south. The Big Four railroad reported it was transporting many of the blacks out of the city.

The soldiers were requested to assist some of the families in their packing. It was learned many of the people had fled the city in such haste all their belongings were left behind.

William Herbert, a black who was interviewed in Macon, Georgia after announcing he was a refugee from the Danville riot, told a reporter the following, "Four years ago after listening to alluring stories told by a Boston Negro of social equality, easy times, and the great love Northerners had for the downtrodden black man, I decided to emigrate to this Eldorado. For nearly four years I have been constantly reminded of the color of my skin and have had all kinds of insults and abuse heaped upon me. I am a bricklayer by trade and although I am considered a good workman, I was ostracized by the unions and was discharged on several occasions because white men would not work with me, and yet they are the same people who make such a howl when a Negro is lynched in the south. All this talk of eating at a white man's table and sitting in the same pew with him in church is hot air." Herbert was described by the reporter as being intelligent and well educated. He told the journalist he intended to spend the rest of his life south of the Ohio River.

August 1st and 2nd was a relatively quiet weekend in the city on the Vermilion River. The riot was still the main topic of conversation as people went about their shopping, but there did not seem to be any organized effort in the making to do anything about the Sheriff or the prisoners in his jail.

The metropolitan newspapers continued to keep their reporters in the city and the news reports they sent out might have come right out of one of the ten cent novels popular during the period. One report stated that hundreds of Vermilion County coal miners would ride into Danville on swift horses and dynamite the jail. This must have been news indeed for the large number of immigrants who worked the mines in the county. They not only did not own "swift horses" but most owned no horses at all. Nearly sixty percent of the miners in the county were from Europe, the largest number being Russians. While stories abounded about what the miners were going to do about the Sheriff and his prisoners, there was never a shred of evidence to indicate they had made a concerted plan to do anything. During the hot summer of 1903, many of the miners were out of work. They would return to the dark shafts once again when the weather turned cold.

Governor Yates was praising the troops for their quick action in moving to Danville. The chief executive was also generous in giving Whitlock credit for defending the county jail. It took the press only the blink of an eye to inform the governor the troops ordered to Danville had arrived after the trouble was over.

The *Danville Press* reported the entire Negro settlement had been in danger of destruction on the night of the riot. A reporter for the paper heard numerous threats that "every Negro in the city" would be killed by morning. He observed a black man and two black women being stoned in a buggy as they traveled on East Main Street during the riot. The mob attempted to stop the trio, but they managed to escape when the man whipped the horse into a run.

Whitlock spent the weekend with his wife and children at the jail. The lawman had received numerous threats against himself and his family. Though he did not ask them to stay at work, his deputies spent much of their off duty time about the jail. The lawmen were a close knit group, and they did not trust the safety of the Sheriff and his family entirely to the soldiers who were standing guard.

August 3rd found the grand jury reconvened with instructions from Judge Thompson to investigate fully the lynching of July 25th, the events leading up to it, and the riot that followed. A few of the men on the grand jury were not comfortable with the situation they found themselves in, but they did not attempt to escape the duty.

The first indictment the jury returned as it met in the massive brick and stone courthouse was against James Wilson. The man who had been the prime target of the rioters at the county jail was indicted for assault.

Whitlock was told to bring the defendant before the judge as soon as possible. The Sheriff and three of his deputies removed Wilson from his cell and walked him from the jail to the courthouse. There was no incident as the four lawmen walked their terrified prisoner across the city square and into the county building. The Sheriff walked in front of Wilson carrying his riot gun and a deputy walked on either side of the prisoner and behind him. The regulars who were sitting on the benches about the building made no remarks as the small procession entered the courthouse.

Wilson was not represented by council as he stood before Judge Thompson and heard the indictment read. When asked for his plea, the young man entered a plea of guilty to assault. Wilson had been wanting to plead guilty since the night of the riot. Judge Thompson sentenced him to an indeterminate period of time to be served at the state penitentiary at Chester, Illinois. The convicted man appeared to be greatly relieved to have the sentencing over. As he and the lawmen made their way back to the county jail, it seemed some of the terror had left him.

In the afternoon Sheriff Whitlock testified before the grand jury.

He was the first of dozens of people who would appear before the investigative body. The reporters waited anxiously in the courthouse hallways to interview the witnesses who had appeared before the jury. They lost no time in stopping those who had testified and asking numerous questions. But the journalists were frustrated, because the witnesses refused to give them any information. When they surrounded State's Attorney Keeslar and asked how the investigation was going, they were told in no uncertain terms he would never grant them an interview.

Governor Yates had now returned to the State Capitol in Springfield, and he was reporting the riot in Danville was the work of anarchists. A reporter working for a paper opposed to the Illinois governor solemnly reported that Governor Richard Yates was a dead "Dickey Bird."

In the stillness of the predawn hours of August 4th, Sheriff Whitlock and his deputies transferred James Wilson from the jail to the C&EI depot. There, Whitlock boarded a train to transport the prisoner to the penitentiary at Chester. While the city of Danville slept, the two men made their last journey together. When Whitlock turned his prisoner over to the officials at the prison, the young man thanked Whitlock for what he had done for him. Though the two men had met only nine days earlier, they would forever be a part of each other's memories and share a moment in history.

While the Sheriff was away, his deputies pulled in another accused rioter. John Robinson of Danville was arrested at his home and was reportedly carrying a number of shot from Whitlock's riot gun in his leg. It was noted his wife had committed suicide a number of years before by burning herself to death. It was alleged she did this because of the treatment she received from Robinson.

August 5th found the grand jury still in session, with no indictments other than the one against James Wilson handed down. Residents were surprised to find Wilson had already been transferred to the Chester penitentiary. As each day passed there were growing signs a significant number of people did not want the rioters prosecuted. The press continued to report the lawbreakers must be prosecuted for the disgrace they had brought to the city, and public figures continued to support the Sheriff. But privately, Whitlock was under increasing pressure to see that any charges brought against the rioters were dropped. As Whitlock listened patiently to those who tried to persuade him to let the rioters go unpunished, he realized he was in a unique situation. While he was unquestionably a hero on the national scene because of his actions on the night of the riot, he found himself to be less than popular in the county which had elected him to office. Many people evidently agreed with one crusty old timer who had stated more than once since the lynching, "the sheriff ought to have his neck stretched."

There were increased rumors an attack would be made on the jail, but these were disregarded as the troops maintained their vigil about the building and in the downtown area. The Sheriff had already demonstrated what he could do with a riot gun, now any attempt to storm the jail would be met with scores of rifles in the hands of trained infantry.

There were a total of ninety men in the two companies of soldiers remaining in the city. They alternated in their duties, one company would do sentry duty and walk patrol while the other company stood down. When a company was off duty, it was put through rigorous training by its officers. This consisted of running several blocks through the city and of doing calisthenics. More than once the troops had marched to the Old Soldiers' Home on the east side of the city. They performed close order drill for the residents and had received a warm reception for their efforts.

Chapter Fifteen

As the midnight hour neared on August 5th, there was activity on the hillside overlooking the river to the south of the jail. The large timber in the wooded areas had been cut years before and now it was covered with scrub trees, weeds, and brambles. A group of silent figures appeared on the dark prominence and began to stealthily climb toward the crest. They spread out in a thin line as they neared the top where their cover thinned to a few sparse bushes.

Private McCallister was standing guard duty at the rear of the jail and his attention was drawn to a movement on the brow of the hill. He quickly brought his rifle up and moved toward the area, calling out a warning as he went.

A short distance east of the jail two soldiers walking patrol spotted a number of figures furtively approaching the militia quarters in the market house. The men shouted an alarm and with rifles at the ready charged the forms. Other soldiers joined the two. Five men sprang up out of the scale yard, which adjoined the market house, and confronted the militia.

Private McCallister noticed a number of shadowy figures advancing on the jail. He pointed his weapon at the nearest form and shouted for the intruder to halt. At the same time alarms were being called out by the militia up and down the line as what appeared to be a skirmish line of attackers, had been located south of the jail. A shower of bricks and rocks were hurled at the soldiers from the brow of the hill as the men there rose to their feet.

A line of the militia was quickly formed up and they faced the unknown number of intruders who had stolen upon their position. The Sheriff had been awakened and alerted to a possible attack, but as quickly as the danger had arisen it disappeared. Faced with a line of ready rifles, the men who had crawled to the crest of the hill now broke and ran into the darkness and safety of the river bottom. The men in the scale yard also retreated when the soldiers advanced toward them. No one was injured by the thrown rocks and bricks and the soldiers did not pursue the men into the river bottom. Sheriff Whitlock, who had joined the soldiers, congratulated them on their vigilance and returned to the jail.

August 6th saw the grand jury hand down twelve indictments against members of the mob that had allegedly attacked the county jail. The question of whether there would be a trial or not had been answered. Word spread swiftly through the city of 25,000 that the first indictments had been returned.

Those who had been boasting of their part in the lynching had been silent since the first arrest was made. Now the men who had been wearing bandages on their wounds made every effort to conceal the evidence of rioting that Sheriff Whitlock's gun had marked them with. Others who had been walking with a noticeable limp and who had explained, when asked, their hobble was because of a wound received at the county jail, seemed to miraculously recover. This caused the saloon keepers to remark, with tongue in cheek, the indictments were the best cure they had ever seen for lameness.

Sherman Cundiff had hired J. B. Mann to represent him at the time of his arrest. Now with the first indictments handed down, the noted attorney would go to work. Mann had a reputation that went beyond the boundaries of the state of Illinois. At one time he had practiced law in Chicago and had been involved in numerous railroad cases.

Born in 1843, Mann would be the oldest attorney involved in the coming trials. He was a graduate of Rutgers University and had studied law under Judge Oliver Davis. He eventually married Judge Davis's daughter and became an intimate member of the Davis family.

His father-in-law had been a close friend of Abraham Lincoln and had tried cases both with Lincoln and opposing him in the courts. It was noted Mann's style in the courtroom reflected that of his teacher, Judge Davis.

Both Mann and Davis had a keen sense of humor, and the son-in-law was never at a loss for a remark. His fondness for an occasional nip on the bottle was well known. He became an instant celebrity among the male population of Danville with a reply he made to a lady who disapproved of his drinking. The woman observed the lawyer exiting a saloon in the morning hours and promptly hailed him. "Mr. Mann," she scolded, "I am surprised to see you coming out of a saloon at this hour of the morning." Mann regarded the lady for a few moments and then questioned her. "Do you expect me to remain in there all day?"

He was a competent attorney who made those opposing him nervous even when his case appeared to be a certain lost cause. But, unlike his father-in-law, he was courteous to his opponents and gracious in his defeats. He often recalled one of the cases where Davis and Lincoln were opposing a railroad attorney in a case. The fiery Davis informed the opposing attorney he and Lincoln would "not only beat you, we will embarrass you." Lincoln quietly informed the other attorney, "Don't mind Oliver." The lanky, future President also reported, "The railroad wasn't embarrassed." This was the background from which Mann had grown to be a very able attorney. He would lead in the effort to have the indictments thrown out. He reportedly confided in one of the other defense attorneys, he didn't think a jury would want to "send any of the boys to prison."

But the men who were pacing the hardwood, plank floors in the Vermilion County jail cells were not as confident as Mann. They were bitter at Whitlock for arresting them, and they lashed out at him verbally for not "supporting white men." Some of the accused wanted to plead guilty and have the matter over with, but on the advice of their lawyers they discarded this idea.

The prisoners decided they had better have a good story to tell when they had to present their defense. The first idea they had concocted was the two mob story. In this account, the first mob stormed the city hall, took Metcalf from his cell in the jail, lynched him, pulled his body over the streets, and then turned the corpse over to a newly formed mob at the county jail. This story sounded so unbelievable it was never given serious consideration. When none of those arrested were accused of the murder of John Metcalf, the two mob story was not needed. The story generally agreed upon was the accused had been drawn to the county jail by the large number of people gathered there. They would testify they were innocent observers, and the fact that some of them had been shot was an unfortunate accident of being in the wrong place when Sheriff Whitlock shot into the mob. As this story was passed from cell to cell, it seemed believable to the growing number of accused rioters who now had residence in the county lockup.

Governor Yates was notified of the trouble at the jail on the previous night and any thoughts that had been considered for withdrawing the troops were abandoned. If the militia had not met the band of men who advanced on the jail under the cover of darkness, there might have been serious trouble. It was rumored the men carried dynamite for breaking into the jail. Whitlock discounted this idea, pointing out the explosives would have blown the arrested rioters to hell along with the others in the jail.

The Sheriff was once again asked to send his wife and children to a safer place, but Laura Whitlock made it clear she would not leave her husband. Whitlock informed Judge Thompson, who had asked him to move his family, he felt there would be no more attacks on the jail. He told the judge his main concern was an impartial jury might not be possible to seat. Whitlock felt it would be nearly impossible to find jurors who would render a verdict of guilty for the rioters. Thompson told the lawman if the mob members came to trial, he would see to it the jury weighed the evidence, not public opinion.

August 7th saw the most vocal of the accused rioters arrested. Detective Halls and Deputy Sheriff Helmick arrested Bessie Dodge at the northeast corner of North and Gobin. Her arrest was the result of a diligent search by the Sheriff's officers. Though they had a good description of the woman and several witnesses had seen her, no one knew her name or where she lived.

The lawmen went to investigate reports that a red headed woman had been threatening the blacks in her neighborhood. When they talked to neighbors of the woman, they learned she had been boasting of her part in the riot. She was still calling for the hanging of the Sheriff. The officers then confronted Dodge. She informed them if she were a man she would show them a few things, but being a woman it was impossible for her to do so. Dodge was charged with being a resident of a "questionable house" until more serious charges could be decided on by the grand jury. Dodge's spirits remained high as she was walked the few blocks to the county jail, but she became noticeably quieter when the steel jail door slammed behind her. Laura Whitlock was called upon to see to the woman's needs. It was a rare occurrence for the Sheriff to have a female prisoner in the jail.

When word spread a woman had been arrested for taking part in the violence of July 25th, the Sheriff was soundly criticized by many. It was rumored he would be arresting the children who had been on the streets the night of the riot next. The lawman did not take any young children into custody, but before the arrests were over, two boys under the age of eighteen would be locked up.

August 8th found one of the youths taken into custody. Sixteen year old Clay Biddle was arrested at 928 Fera Street. He had a flesh wound in his knee and it was thought to have been caused by Whitlock's shotgun. Biddle had no money for bond and was placed in jail with the others who had been arrested in connection with the riot.

Whitlock was still receiving large numbers of letters from individuals and resolutions from other cities commending him for his actions at the jail. But at home the praise was not as lavish. A businessman called upon the Sheriff and one of his advisors in the afternoon. As the acquaintances sat in the cramped quarters of the Sheriff's office, the man chastised Whitlock for the way he was handling the investigation.

While the jail house clock mechanically called off the seconds from its place on the wall, Whiltlock listened in silence to the man facing him. The Sheriff was told that by arresting people he was giving the newspapers more fodder for their sensational stories. He was continuing to darken the name of Danville. It was pointed out if the rioters had really intended to harm the Sheriff or his family on the night of the riot, they could certainly have done so. The man told Whitlock the rioters had been shooting in the air not at the jail or any individuals. He then told the lawman he had to make a choice and it appeared he was taking the side of the Negroes against the whites. The businessman concluded this was a serious mistake for a man in political office to make.

Whilock regarded his visitor for a few seconds and then slowly stood, his big hands jammed in his pockets. His guest grew uneasy as the silence continued and the Sheriff's face seemed to darken. The lawman then broke the silence and replied to each of the points the other man had made. It wasn't a matter of race, it was a matter of law and order, Whitlock pointed out. He stated he had taken the job to uphold the law and that was what he was going to do, let the chips fall where they would. As for the rioters shooting in the air, the lawman informed his visitor he had bullet holes in the windows of the jail to prove the shots were not aimed upwards. The Sheriff further pointed out many of the men who were shooting had been drinking heavily. He asked his visitor if he would tolerate a drunk shooting in his direction and then believe the man if he explained he had been shooting to miss? The lawman concluded he was going to do his duty, and it would be up to a judge and jury to decide the guilt or innocence of those he was arresting.

When the man left the county jail, he took with him what all the others had taken who had tried to persuade Sheriff Hardy Whitlock to drop his investigation into the riot; the assurance nothing, short of death, was going to make the lawman end his investigation and pursuit of the rioters.

City Hall, Danville, IL., 1903, 24 North Walnut Street. This building, built in 1896, housed city police headquarters, the holdover for city prisoners, police magistrate offices, city council and alderman meeting rooms, and the mayor's office.

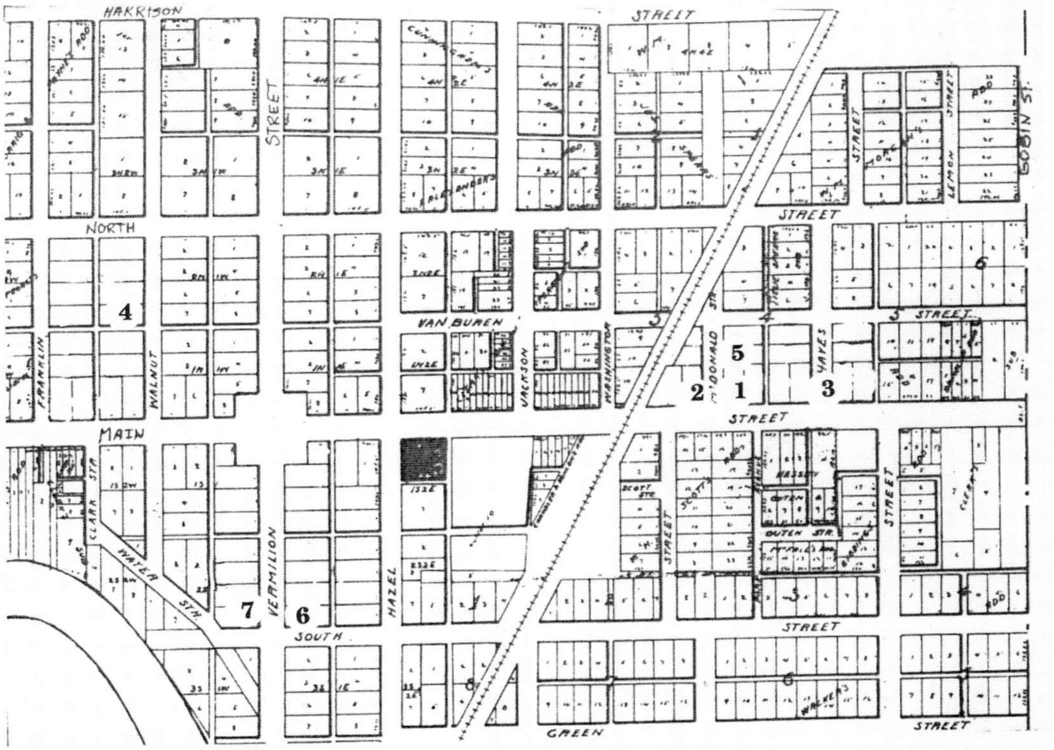

City Site Map of Danville

1. Shermayer's Saloon
2. Gatterman shot
3. Metcalf captured
4. City Hall
5. Metcalf hung by mob.
6. Body cremated by mob
7. County jail

Aetna House, Danville, IL, corner of North Vermilion and North Streets.

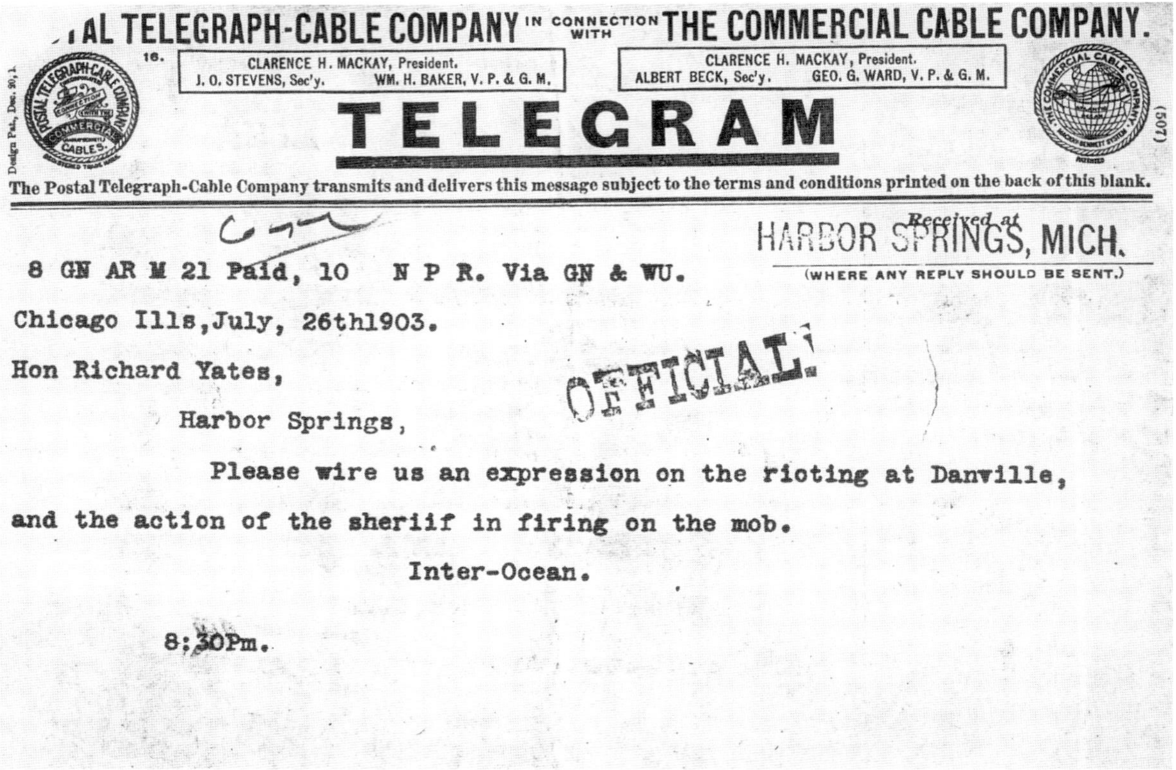

...AL TELEGRAPH-CABLE COMPANY IN CONNECTION WITH THE COMMERCIAL CABLE COMPANY.

16. CLARENCE H. MACKAY, President. J. O. STEVENS, Sec'y. WM. H. BAKER, V. P. & G. M.

CLARENCE H. MACKAY, President. ALBERT BECK, Sec'y. GEO. G. WARD, V. P. & G. M.

(507)

Design Pat., Dec. 20, 1.

TELEGRAM

The Postal Telegraph-Cable Company transmits and delivers this message subject to the terms and conditions printed on the back of this blank.

Received at HARBOR SPRINGS, MICH.
(WHERE ANY REPLY SHOULD BE SENT.)

8 GN AR M 21 Paid, 10 N P R. Via GN & WU.

Chicago Ills, July, 26th1903.

Hon Richard Yates,

Harbor Springs,

OFFICIAL

Please wire us an expression on the rioting at Danville, and the action of the sheriff in firing on the mob.

Inter-Ocean.

8:30Pm.

Telegram received from news service "Inter-Ocean" requesting information about the rioting in Danville, IL.

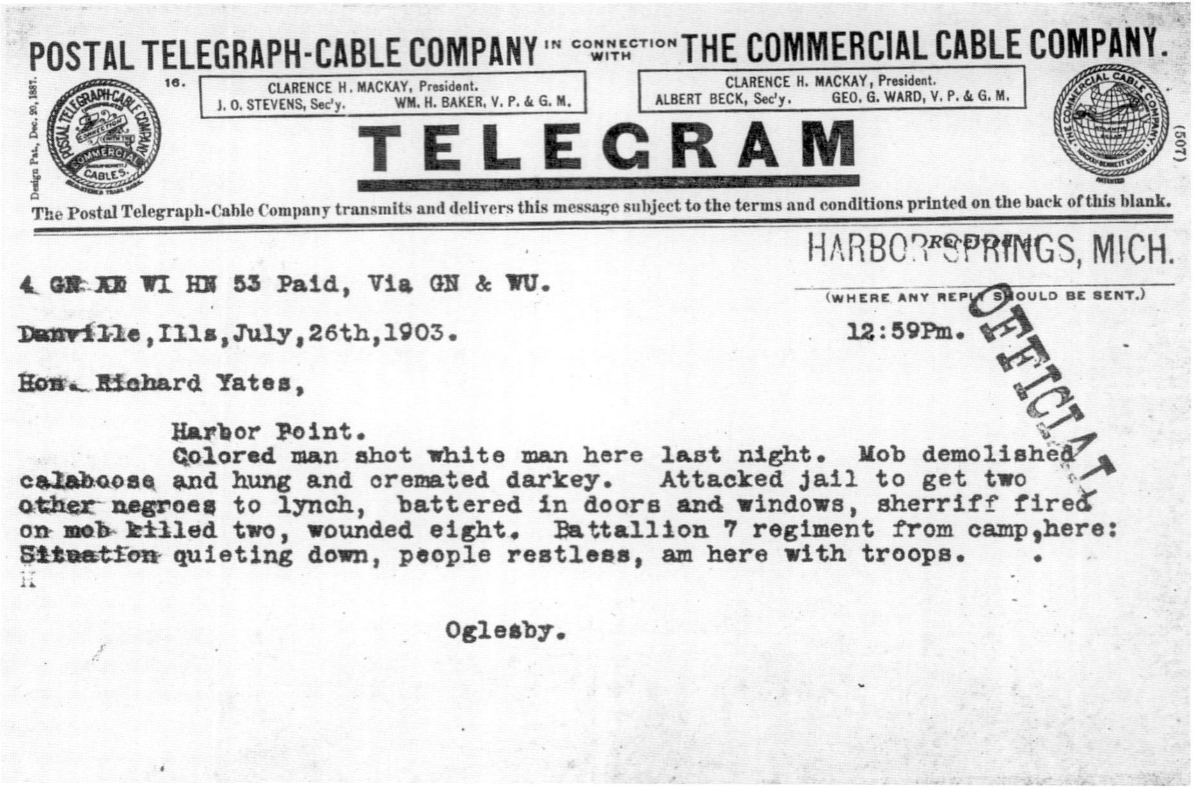

POSTAL TELEGRAPH-CABLE COMPANY IN CONNECTION WITH THE COMMERCIAL CABLE COMPANY.

Design Pat., Dec. 20, 1887.

16.

CLARENCE H. MACKAY, President.
J. O. STEVENS, Sec'y. WM. H. BAKER, V. P. & G. M.

CLARENCE H. MACKAY, President.
ALBERT BECK, Sec'y. GEO. G. WARD, V. P. & G. M.

(507)

TELEGRAM

The Postal Telegraph-Cable Company transmits and delivers this message subject to the terms and conditions printed on the back of this blank.

HARBOR SPRINGS, MICH.

(WHERE ANY REPLY SHOULD BE SENT.)

OFFICIAL

4 GN XE WI HN 53 Paid, Via GN & WU.

Danville, Ills, July, 26th, 1903. 12:59Pm.

Hon. Richard Yates,

Harbor Point.

Colored man shot white man here last night. Mob demolished calaboose and hung and cremated darkey. Attacked jail to get two other negroes to lynch, battered in doors and windows, sherriff fired on mob killed two, wounded eight. Battallion 7 regiment from camp, here: Situation quieting down, people restless, am here with troops.

Oglesby.

Telegram sent from the governor's personal secretary, Colonel Oglesby, giving him details of the problems in Danville, IL.

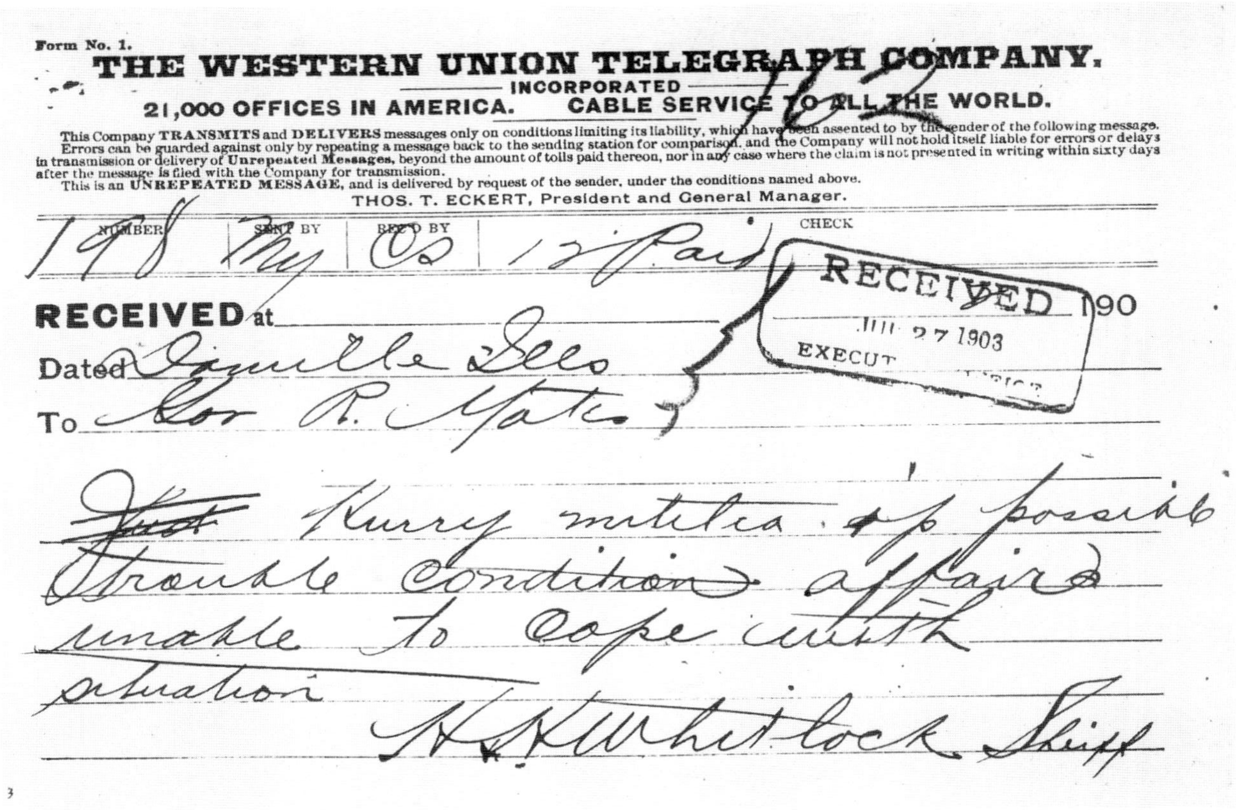
Form No. 1.

THE WESTERN UNION TELEGRAPH COMPANY.

INCORPORATED

21,000 OFFICES IN AMERICA. CABLE SERVICE TO ALL THE WORLD.

This Company TRANSMITS and DELIVERS messages only on conditions limiting its liability, which have been assented to by the sender of the following message. Errors can be guarded against only by repeating a message back to the sending station for comparison, and the Company will not hold itself liable for errors or delays in transmission or delivery of Unrepeated Messages, beyond the amount of tolls paid thereon, nor in any case where the claim is not presented in writing within sixty days after the message is filed with the Company for transmission.

This is an UNREPEATED MESSAGE, and is delivered by request of the sender, under the conditions named above.

THOS. T. ECKERT, President and General Manager.

NUMBER	SENT BY	REC'D BY	CHECK
198	My	Os	13 Paid

RECEIVED at 190

RECEIVED JUL 27 1903 EXECUT

Dated Danville Ills

To Gov R. Yates

~~Just~~ Hurry militia if possible trouble condition affairs unable to cope with situation

H. K. Whitlock Sheriff

Telegram from Sheriff Whitlock to Governor Yates asking for troops to help handle the situation in Danville, IL.

Vermilion County Jail, 1903, 38-40 South Vermilion Street, Danville, IL.

John W. Keeslar, State's Attorney, who was prosecuting attorney for the trials.

Vermilion County Courthouse, corner of Main and Vermilion Streets, Danville, IL.

GEO. T. BUCKINGHAM,
ATTORNEY AT LAW.
304-305 DANIEL BUILDING,
DANVILLE, ILLINOIS.

RECEIVED
JUL 30 1903
EXECUTIVE OFFICE.

July 29, 1903.
JUL 31 1903

My dear Governor:-

Pursuant to the communication with your office this afternoon by telephone, I beg to say that at a conference with the Circuit Judge, States Attorney and Sheriff this afternoon, I was requested to suggest to you the advisability of keeping the two companies, or at least one company, here for some days longer.

It is the impression among the officers, and practically all of the substantial citizens who are backing them up, that the Sheriff would have no trouble in keeping the situation in hand, but it is believed that the presence of the troops during the events of the next ten days will have a repressive influence, which might prevent a possible further outbreak.

The program now agreed on is to reconvene the grand jury next Monday morning, indict the mob leaders and immediately summons a special petit jury, and place them on trial. It is, of course, just possible that because of these wholesale arrests and the prompt prosecutions which will follow, there might arise further disturbances, and particularly is this true on next Saturday night.

You, of course, are aware that we have here a very mixed population, including several thousand coal miners of divers nationalities. To add to the gravity of the situation here, the mayor and the city administration are utterly inefficient to maintain order.

First page of letter sent to Governor Yates by George T. Buckingham encouraging the governor to keep troops in Danville, IL, longer than originally anticipated.

Vermilion County Circuit Judge Morton W. Thompson, a Vermilion County native from Fithian, IL.

Called "Vermilion County's Wyatt Earp," in this *Commercial-News* picture, Sheriff Hardy Whitlock is shown (third from left, front row) in front of the county jail with members of a grand jury. Note the Whitlock children on the porch.

Chapter Sixteen

August 10th was the day a summons was issued for Mayor John Beard to appear before the grand jury. Beard had reportedly been in city hall at the time the mob began to gather in front of the building. A number of statements had been credited to the Mayor concerning the riot, but there was no confirmation from him that he had made any of them. It was reported the order for the city police not to shoot at the rioters had been issued by Beard. The grand jury would ask the leader of the city why a large, well armed police force, with a loaded riot gun hanging on the wall, could not stop rioters as Sheriff Whitlock had done. They pointed out the Sheriff had stopped a much larger mob with a smaller force.

This was also the day a letter written by Sheriff Whitlock to Governor Yates was made public. The chief executive of Illinois had asked the Sheriff to write him a letter with suggestions about how such incidents as the riot could be better handled in the future. Whitlock's missive was highly critical of Yates for leaving the state and not placing someone on duty in Springfield when he was absent, especially during a period when there had been racial problems and a recent lynching in the state.

The governor's aides immediately rebuked Whitlock for the strong language of his letter and for releasing its contents to the press before it was in Yates's hands. A number of Republican newspapers also criticized the Sheriff for his method of reprimanding the governor. Some newsmen implied Whitlock was trying to make political hay at the expense of Yates.

The Democratic papers greeted the flap between Whitlock, who was now viewed by many as a hero, and Yates, who they had already pronounced a dead "Dickey Bird," with glee. One paper reported the Sheriff had fired another shot down the rail and this one had hit a target in Springfield.

Whitlock's letter also pointed out local governments should be more attentive to the needs of their law enforcement agencies. He noted when he had asked the Vermilion County Board to purchase a riot gun for his department, he had been informed such a weapon was unnecessary. The gun that stopped the riot on July 25th in Danville was purchased with the Sheriff's own funds.

The exodus of blacks from the city of Danville had slowed by the second week of August, but a significant number of the minority population had left the city by that date. One who did not leave was Louisa Myers, who lived just south of city hall on Walnut Street. Myers had watched the mob from her home as they gathered at the city building, and she had seen them take Metcalf from the police.

She now asked a city employee who was repairing a brush on the curb in front of her home to do it elsewhere. The man called out to the police who were nearby and said the woman had threatened him and called him names. Myers was placed under arrest and taken before Justice Custer. The Justice was informed that Myers had been causing trouble since the lynching. She had reportedly had problems with Joe Long, the owner of the feed yard where the rope came from that was used to hang Metcalf. Custer fined the woman $7.40 and told her not to cause any further problems. Myers paid her fine and was released from custody.

August 12th was the day the grand jury finished its investigation into the riot. The group of men had spent six days hearing testimony and discussing the violence of July 25th. They handed down a number of indictments. The total number of individuals indicted for the mob action at the jail reached twenty-four.
Those indicted were Winfield Baker, Bessie Dodge alias Bessie Armstrong, Clay Biddle, Thomas Bell, Edward Hart, Adam Murray, William Redwine, Isaac Newton Slade, John Robertson, John "Jack" Walton, Francis Cicero Davis, William Pettis, Clements Mobaker, Sherman Cundiff, Richard Roberts, John Isom, Harry Rennick, Benjamin Govin, 0l Manifield, Charles E. Rost, Charles Devore, John Kress, Horace Murphy, and Harvey VanGundy.

Many vocations were represented by those indicted. There were eight miners, two farm laborers, an electrician, a carpenter, a construction worker, two clerks, a saloon worker, two railroad men, a laborer, a teamster, two unemployed, a prostitute, and one whose occupation was unknown.

When the names of those indicted reached the public, there was a further outcry from many people. Though some of those indicted were not well known in the county, others had family and friends who lashed out at the grand jury for its findings. Many had believed the accused rioters would be released from jail after a few days, now the word prison was being heard when the future of those arrested was discussed. A number of new threats were made against the Sheriff at this time, and Deputy Newlin advised Whitlock to take the warnings seriously. The lawman commented he would not be intimidated and told the deputy the arrests would continue.

Shortly after noon on the 12th, Whitlock and a lawyer, who was his friend and adviser, received a committee of businessmen at the jail. As he found chairs for the men to sit on in his sparsely furnished office, he could tell by their faces they did not come to praise him for the indictments that had just been returned.

A spokesman for the group told the Sheriff they were of the opinion the troops should be withdrawn. They felt the continued presence of armed militia in their city was casting a bad reflection on Danville. They further felt the approaching trial was a total waste of time and taxpayer money, and would be a further source of embarrassment to a city which had received more than its share of bad headlines. They pointed out to the Sheriff many people thought the "poor devils" who had been struck by his buckshot and who had been locked up in jail, had suffered enough.

Whitlock listened patiently to the men, as he had done with the many others who had tried to curtail the investigation into the riot. The men explained Danville was usually a law abiding place and in many ways a model city. The last thing they made clear to the quiet lawman was the political facts of life; to survive in politics, he was told, he must learn to compromise. One of the men noted the Sheriff wasn't making many friends by "not standing up for white men."

Whitlock was just beginning to respond to the men when two of his deputies brought a man to the door of his office. The individual the deputies had under arrest was William Shuey, and he walked with a noticeable limp. Deputy Newlin explained to Whitlock they had arrested the man at his home, and it appeared he had picked up a few buckshot in his foot. Shuey told the Sheriff he would be able to make bail. Whitlock told his men to take the arrested man before a justice of the peace.

The committee of businessmen silently followed Shuey and the arresting officers out of the jail. The deputies had provided the answer to their plea, the arrests would go on.

The Sheriff wasn't the only one being pressured. Similar appeals had been made to Judge Thompson and State's Attorney Keeslar, and those two individuals had also rebuffed those who would side-track the Sheriff's actions.

Pressure applied on Governor Yates to remove the troops from Danville was having a more profound effect. A number of wires were being sent back and forth between Danville and the state capitol in Springfield. Governor Yates was careful to word his messages in a manner that would absolve him of any responsibility for any trouble which might occur after the troops were removed. He was feeling the pressure to recall the militia.

August 15th was the day the commander of the troops in Danville responded to the order to remove his troops from the city. Captain Frank Biggs had replaced Colonel Clasby as commanding officer of the Seventh Regiment units in the city. Biggs now sent his own wire over the Western Union lines to Springfield.

August 15 Danville, Illinois
Gov. Richard Yates, Springfield, Ills.
Received orders report home; think mistake. Opinion troops should remain. Man murdered Tuesday night; strong feeling against murderer. Miners excited.
Frank J. Biggs, Capt.

The incident the army officer was referring to was the shooting of hotel clerk Cornelius Boyle by Joe Cummins. Contrary to what Biggs reported, Boyle was not killed in the incident, but so critically wounded it was thought he would die. The assailant, referred to as "drunken Joe," was being held in a state of limbo in the county jail. The decision was made not to charge him until the clerk had either succumbed to his wound or shown some improvement.

In the saloons of the city there was talk of lynching Cummins if Boyle died. But friends of Joe pointed out, since he had been so drunk he could not recall shooting the clerk, a lynching seemed uncalled for. The debate over the lynching died out when Boyle took a turn for the better and it was reported he would live.

Chapter Seventeen

August 17th was the first day a reporter was allowed in the county jail by Sheriff Whitlock to interview one of the prisoners. The journalist asked that Bessie Dodge be the subject of his interview and the lawman granted the request.

The newsman found Dodge in a cell in the north cell block of the jail. A section of the area had been set aside to give her a bit of privacy away from the male prisoners. Laura Whitlock had provided the woman with a few items of comfort that made the small room a little less stark. One of them was a tiny footed mirror that stood on a washstand the Sheriff's wife had moved into the cell.

When told she had the distinction of being the first woman in the history of the county to be charged with inciting a riot, Dodge stoutly denied she deserved the charge. As she sat on the small cot that took up a large portion of her tiny prison, Dodge gave her version of what had happened on Saturday night.

She and a male escort had been strolling about the streets and had decided to attend the Indian Show at the public square. They had hardly arrived there when the mob begin to push its way through the square on its way to the county jail. She related she and her friend had followed along, at a distance, to observe the expected excitement. She admitted she had criticized the Sheriff for shooting white men to protect the Negro prisoners in his custody, but she defiantly stated she had a right to such an opinion.

When the journalist asked Dodge what her defense would be, the woman seemed to be less sure of herself. She said she would make the best defense possible, but she had no money to hire a good lawyer. Further, due to her profession, she would not be able to use her male friend as an alibi because to do so would "give him away."

The journalist declared Dodge to be exceedingly cheerful for someone behind bars awaiting trial. When Whitlock was asked by the reporter if he could interview Baker, the alleged leader of the mob, the request was denied.

August 18th was the day of arraignment for the rioters. A huge crowd was gathered for the legal proceedings in the county courthouse. Others waited outside the county building to see the prisoners as they were marched from the jail to their place of arraignment. The military had offered to provide an escort, but Whitlock had declined the offer, explaining to Captain Biggs it would be better if the legal proceedings were handled by local authorities.

At mid-morning, the door to the jail opened and Sheriff Whitlock and a number of deputies brought out the men to be arraigned. Bessie Dodge was not among the silent group as they filed out of the building into the bright sunlight. When reporters asked where the red headed woman was, they were informed she would be taken to court later in the day.

The men were all handcuffed and remained silent as they made their way the short block to the courthouse at the northeast corner of Vermilion and Main Streets. Most of them had been locked up for nearly three weeks and their skin had lost much of its summer tan. They stared down or straight ahead as they were herded along Vermilion Street by the lawmen. When friends and acquaintances called out to the prisoners, they were answered with a nod or a resigned shake of a head. The wounds some of the men had received from Whitlock's shotgun hindered their ability to move very rapidly.

The prisoners entered single file through the south door of the county building and made their way up the stairs to the second story courtroom. The room was full of people and many more were lined up along the walls of the corridors leading to the room. As the prisoners were ushered to their seats, there were calls of greeting from individuals in the crowded room. The noise level in the courtroom increased steadily as the prisoners began to visit with relatives and friends in the packed chamber. When Judge Thompson entered, there was a slight drop in the clamor as the assemblage rose to acknowledge his presence.

Thompson lost no time in calling the names of those indicted. As each man was asked for his plea, the reply remained the same, not guilty. Whitlock quietly watched the proceedings from a seat behind his prisoners. Deputies were near the men and at the rear of the courtroom. They stood guard at the doors which provided entrance to the courthouse. There was also a squad of soldiers at the market house ready to report to the Sheriff if there was a call for help. But the proceedings were going smoothly and it did not appear there would be any trouble. Whitlock had to endure the hard looks he was given by the friends and families of those being arraigned, but the lawman's expression gave no indication he was bothered by the stares. He was also the object of a number of caustic remarks, but he did not respond to the jibes. The Sheriff had already told his deputies they should expect such remarks and not to be prodded into doing something irrational.

When the name of Edward Hart was called, there was silence in the courtroom as the young miner failed to respond. After his name was called three times the court waited a brief period, but the man still did not respond. When Judge Thompson proceeded to another man, Hart's father, a miner living near Oakwood, approached Sheriff Whitlock.

The elder Hart, who was an acquaintance of the Sheriff, explained his son had left the country and would not be returning. He had left at his mother's request. She had told the young man she could not stand the thought of him being in jail or prison. The bond Hart's father had put up would be forfeited. This represented a major financial sacrifice at a time when the average wage was less than $15 per week.

When Winfield Baker entered his plea of not guilty, the Kentuckian also informed the court he would like to defend himself. The tall, slender Baker stated he had once studied law for four months and was confident he could handle his own case. Judge Thompson granted the request but warned the Kentuckian he thought he might be making a mistake.

After all the prisoners had entered pleas of not guilty, they were escorted back to their cells at the county jail. On the return trip down Vermilion Street the men seemed to lose some of their quietness and responded to the calls being made to them as they walked along under the watchful eyes of Whitlock and his deputies.

A number of lawyers would be representing the rioters in the coming trial. In addition to J. B. Mann there would be W. L. Cundiff, the firm of Mabin and Schecter, Charles Taylor, W. R.

Chambers, George W. Salmons, Charles E. Brown, A. B. Dennis, and William Beckwith. Judge Thompson had appointed Dennis, Salmons, Brown, and Beckwith to defend those who could not afford an attorney.

The defense attorneys were a talented group of men. Mann, Mabin, and Salmons were all members of the group that had founded the Vermilion County Bar Association. They shared that distinction with Judge Thompson and State's Attorney Keeslar. Salmons and Mann had both served in the Illinois State Legislature and A. B. Dennis would do so in the future. Mann was Danville's first city attorney and Dennis would become the first assistant attorney general in Springfield. If the rioters were convicted, it would not be because they did not have capable defense representation.

Confronting this august group would be John Keeslar, who had little in common with the opposing attorneys except the practice of law. Keeslar did not drink, smoke, or have any other vices that had ever been discovered. It was observed if he had a sense of humor, he kept it well concealed. There could not have been a greater disparity in the personalities of two men than there were in State's Attorney Keeslar, who would prosecute, and attorney Mann, who would organize the early defense.

Bessie Dodge was escorted to the courtroom in the afternoon and entered a plea of not guilty in a firm voice. Laura Whitlock had seen to it that Dodge obtained one of her better dresses for the court appearance, and one of the reporters present remarked she was almost attractive.

In 1903 it was a man's world, and Dodge was somewhat of an anomaly. It was a time when women were denied most of the basic rights men took for granted. They did not vote, could not hold public office, could not own property in many places, and were discriminated against in the work place. They were expected to keep any opinions they had to themselves or at least confine them to the privacy of their own homes. If they did express themselves in a public manner, they were more often than not treated with ridicule and branded as "brazen hussies."

Dodge had the audacity to remark that women should be allowed to serve on a jury. She informed her attorney if she were truly to be tried by her peers, women should be included. This remark by the defendant was passed around the legal circle and provided a good laugh for those who heard it. A number of the men agreed the woman definitely did not know her place.

Judge Thompson set August 21st for the date he would hear arguments from the defense to have the indictments thrown out. This seemed to some of the rioters their best hope of being set free. The predicament of those indicted was best expressed by Isaac Slade. He remarked, "We were guilty as hell and the Judge knew it, the attorneys on both sides knew it and anyone with an ounce of common sense could figure it out." One of the first tasks the defense attorneys had was convincing their clients to plead innocent. Then, they had to keep them from changing their pleas because some were under the misconception that since they were guilty, they should plead that way.

The defense attorneys explained that if one of those indicted entered a plea of guilty, it would hurt the chances of all the others. The rioters who had been arraigned were assured by their lawyers there was a fair chance they would never have to stand trial. They expected the indictments to be thrown out. Slade did not have a lot of confidence the charges would be dismissed, and he had even less hope a jury would find him innocent. He had resigned himself to "the worst" and was expecting jail.

Part 3

The Trial

Chapter Eighteen

The dog days of August held Vermilion County in a firm grasp as preparations were made for the trials of the rioters. Along the roadways and railroad right of ways the late summer wild flowers were forecasting the coming of autumn as they nodded their colorful blooms at those passing by.

In the jail, the prisoners waited for the coming trial as did Whitlock and his deputies. The Sheriff had little to do with the rioters who were lodged in his jail, but a few of the deputies would visit with the arrested men when they had spare time. Bessie Dodge was left to Laura Whitlock. The Sheriff's wife felt sympathetic toward the woman accused of participating in the violence at the county jail.

The saloons in the city continued to do a booming business and were the source of many alcohol induced plans for "rescuing" the arrested men from jail. In the sober light of day these plans disappeared along with the hangover from the night before. The church leaders, many of the women of the city, and a few of the law enforcement people wanted something done about the unregulated drinking in Danville, but their complaints fell on deaf ears. The women would have their say in 1916 when, in their first trip to the ballot box, they would vote the city dry.

Attorney Buckingham had informed Governor Yates that, in his opinion, the mayor and city administration were "utterly inefficient to maintain order." He also informed the chief executive of the state two members of the police force were professional gamblers and others were of the "criminal class." He softened his criticism of the city police by noting some of the men were "good officers." It was partially this lack of faith in the local city police department which encouraged the governor to leave troops in the city of Danville.

L. Perry Cookingham, who was a young boy at the time of the

lynching, would have some profound memories of early twentieth century Danville. The man, who became the premier city manager in the nation by rescuing Kansas City, Missouri from the ravages of the Pendergast machine, grew up in Danville, IL.

He remarked Danville was about as corrupt as a small city could be. A change in the mayor and city council usually meant the firing of most of the policemen, firemen, and other employees who were not lined up with the newly elected officials.

Cookingham observed further that Danville's citizens could expect little from the city except a few days before election. Then, maybe, the weeds would get cut along the unpaved streets and occasionally the horse-drawn grader would smooth out the ruts left in the mud by the spring thaw. The man who rebuilt Kansas City also remarked on the electoral process in Danville. In the poverty areas of the city, paper slips would be handed out to the voters. A slip would inform the prospective vote caster that if a certain candidate won, two dollars could be received at a given address by producing the slip with the message.

Judge Morton Thompson noted what "really rankled" a few of the people in Danville was their inability to control the Sheriff. Danville, like many similar sized places of its time, had a number of citizens who were adept at "controlling things." They looked upon themselves as the "guardians" of a certain image. This image was not enhanced when a large part of the population of the city went mad and murdered and butchered a human being on the streets. The fact he might have been a murderer did not make the barbarous behavior of the citizens any more acceptable. In Danville, the judge noted, it was a common practice to try to sweep the "dirt" under the bed. It was a shock to many of those who thought they ran things when they discovered Whitlock would not be their "broom." This was the political environment, as perceived by some, existing in Danville in 1903.

If Whitlock and Keeslar were the least bit intimidated by the pressure they were under to go easy on the rioters, they never let it show. Both men were determined to see the indicted persons stand trial and be found guilty. The greatest concern the two men had was the possibility of a friend, or friends of those indicted, ending up on the trial jury. The two men who represented the law were told repeatedly their political careers would be over if they persisted in the prosecution of the rioters.

August 21st was the day arguments were heard for the quashing of the indictments against the accused. A huge crowd once again gathered in and around the courthouse for the proceedings.

Mixed in with the large number of buggies and rigs parked on the downtown streets were a scattering of the new horseless carriages. Though the first automobile had made its appearance in Danville on May 24, 1896, the odd appearing conveyances were still an object of curiosity.

Defense Attorney Joseph B. Mann arrived at the courthouse in a motorcar. Though the noted attorney did not personally drive the vehicle, the fact he used one made some of the locals, who had condemned autos as a passing fad, take note. A number of citizens gathered around Mann's vehicle to examine it as they waited for the court proceedings to begin.

Mann was of medium height with a well trimmed white beard and mustache. His hat was pushed firmly down on his head. He gave the reporters clustered around the entrance to the courthouse a look which discouraged them from firing questions at him. But, in characteristic fashion, he turned when he reached the door to the building and told the newsmen he would have a statement after the arguments were made. The attorney realized the press could either be a strong ally or a powerful foe.

Mann's son, Oliver, would watch his father in the courtroom. The younger Mann had been admitted to the bar in 1903 and was a member of his father's law firm. In April of 1916 Oliver Mann would make a trip to Springfield and meet with Illinois Governor Dunne to plead the case of John Murphy, a black convicted of murder and sentenced to hang. Oliver Mann would succeed in obtaining a stay of execution and appeal Murphy's conviction. The appeal would fail and the man would be put to death in the Vermilion County jail in February of 1917.

Judge Thompson's courtroom was again filled to overflowing when court convened. The defendants, and their families and friends, filled a large portion of the room. Sheriff Whitlock once again took a seat behind those indicted and remained silent. A large press contingent was on hand. The reporters scribbled notes on their small pads as they attempted to question some of the participants in the proceedings. A few women were present in the crowded room, but they were only a small minority of the observers. Clay Biddle's mother was present and wore an anguished look, as she would at every court appearance her son made.

Watchful deputies once again took up positions at the doors to the courthouse. They were vigilant for any signs of trouble from friends of those arrested. But the mood of the people remained one of curiosity. If there was to be trouble, the lawmen expected it to come under cover of darkness.

Judge Thompson succeeded in bringing the noise in the courtroom down to an acceptable level. Mann and Attorney Cundiff were ready to state the case for the defendants. Mann confided to one of the other defense attorneys that if the indictments were not thrown out it would be hard to get an acquittal in a jury trial.

The defense attorneys informed the court the indictments were poorly drawn and had been written in haste. Mann displayed his considerable courtroom ability, and it was clear he was having an affect on those who were watching. He showed sadness that a group of fine citizens could be indicted, randomly, from a crowd of thousands. He was angry a grand jury had given credence to the papers drawn up by a state's attorney who evidently wanted to see someone pay for the violence that occurred in Danville, whether they were guilty or not.

The defense attorneys pounced on the wording of one indictment with a show of indignation that such a legal document could ever reach a courtroom. They pointed out the statutes required either thirty persons unarmed or twelve persons armed be named in an indictment before they could legally be charged with assembling for the purpose of civil disobedience. Mann contended the state had not met either of these criteria. State's Attorney Keeslar did not argue the point because it was clear in the indictments he had not met these two points of law. The defendants exchanged knowing glances as Mann and Cundiff seemed to be making points in their favor.

The defense attacked the indictment for assault with intent to commit murder with outrage. This was the charge guaranteed to garner the accused a prison sentence if they were convicted. The attorneys contended each of the accused should have been named in a separate indictment, and also, each of the people they planned to assault should have been named individually. The legal papers had named as a group the accused and the four men they were planning to lynch.

Prosecutor Keeslar was not intimidated by the fiery delivery of Mann. He slowly paced in front of the bench defending his indictments in a quiet manner. He pointed out the defendants had committed the alleged crime at one and the same time and as a body. He gave examples from numerous authorities to support his argument. As the two sides debated the legality of the indictments, the courtroom became increasingly more silent as spectators and family tried to weigh the effect of the attorneys' words on Judge Thompson.

The arguments took most of the day and the heat in the packed courtroom was stifling. Defendant Bessie Dodge became ill during the afternoon and had to be returned to her jail cell. Winfield Baker remained cheerful and visited with the other accused who were lined up in the dock. Jack Walton, a favorite of the trial observers, exchanged good humored remarks with those near him. But most of the other defendants remained silent and wore a concerned expression.

The reporters observed Mann and Cundiff had made points with the trial watchers with their arguments. Judge Thompson had remained impassive during the long presentation. They also noted, while Mann and Cundiff both exhibited considerable flair in their arguments, such a performance was most effective on a jury, not on a judge. The slender Keeslar, on the other hand, had presented his defense of the indictments in a calm manner. His voice was hardly audible to those in the back of the room.

It was growing late in the afternoon when the attorneys finished their arguments over the indictments. Judge Thompson regarded the men facing him for a few seconds before he began to render his decision. The low hum of conversation taking place among the observers dropped to a few discreet whispers and all waited for Mort Thompson to speak.

The judge upheld the indictments, dismissing three counts only. He agreed with the defense. There were not thirty persons unarmed or twelve persons armed named in the indictments. This small victory saw the charge of assembling for civil disobedience thrown out. But the day belonged to the prosecution, and Keeslar gave Sheriff Whitlock a satisfied nod as the two prepared to leave the courtroom. The serious indictments had all withstood the challenge of the defense and had not been touched. Now the door was open to send the rioters to prison if a jury could be convinced of their guilt.

Judge Thompson set Monday, August 24th as the day for the first trial. Winfield Baker would be the first to face a jury. The Kentuckian had been indicted individually for the assault and attempted murder of Sheriff Whitlock. As the Sheriff and his deputies marched the prisoners back to the county jail, Whitlock was the target of a number of jeers from friends of the accused. The Sheriff ignored his detractors, but the deputies moved toward those who were shouting, and the small gathering that had been causing the disturbance broke up.

Chapter Nineteen

August 24th saw the largest crowd yet assembled gathered at the courthouse. There was not room in the courtroom for all the spectators, so many contented themselves with filling the benches, banisters, ledges, and any other surface providing a seat in and around the county building. A number of soldiers were on the south side of the building and remained there until the Sheriff and two of his deputies had brought Baker to the courthouse. Once the prisoner was safely inside, the squad of armed soldiers moved off and deputies took up a post at the south and west entrances to the building.

The morning was spent in selecting a jury, a task proving more difficult with each ensuing trial. Since Baker was not a native of Vermilion County, he did not have a large number of friends or acquaintances in the area. When Judge Thompson adjourned for noon, a jury was on hand and ready to hear the evidence in the Baker trial.

At 1:00 P.M. Judge Thompson took his chair and the trial began. Attorneys Salmons and Brown were on hand to represent Baker; Keeslar would prosecute for the state.

Baker was in excellent spirits as he sat in the defendant's chair. He exchanged remarks with those within hearing range. The journalists scribbled down notes as the Kentuckian with the drooping mustache shot some of his comments in their direction. Keeslar sat quietly and drummed his fingers lightly on the small table holding his briefs. Salmons and Brown were engaged in conversation and gave the jury a few contemplative glances as they exchanged remarks.

Judge Thompson regarded the packed courtroom warily and

quieted the noisy spectators as Sheriff Whitlock was called to the witness stand. The noise in the room subsided somewhat as the lawman took his seat in the witness chair.

Whitlock was sworn in and State's Attorney Keeslar slowly walked to the front of the courtroom. The thin attorney had his hands clasped behind his back and he seemed to be studying the courtroom floor. He asked Whitlock if he saw the man in the room who had attempted to kill him on the night of July 25th.

Whitlock responded by saying yes. When asked to identify the man, the lawman raised his arm and pointed at Baker. The Kentuckian showed no change in emotion as the Sheriff's eyes met his. A smile seemed to tug at his lips as the two faced each other. Whitlock's expression remained stern and it was Baker who dropped his eyes first.

When the prosecutor asked the Sheriff to relate what happened on the night of July 25th, the lawman testified in a calm manner, his deep voice filling the courtroom. Once again he pointed at the Kentuckian, who was sitting quietly beside attorney Salmons, and related how Baker had attempted to kill him on the night of the riot.

Whitlock said he had seen the defendant clearly, as Baker pulled a revolver and fired in his direction. He related the Kentuckian had made threats against those in the jail and had told the lawman that someone would be killed if he did not give up the prisoners. He noted Baker had repeatedly called for the mob to attack the jail during the course of the evening.

As the sad eyes of a beardless Abraham Lincoln stared down from a framed picture on the wall of the courtroom, Attorney Salmons approached Sheriff Whitlock to begin the cross examination.

He asked the lawman if he had ever seen the defendant before the alleged crime took place at the jail. Whitlock replied that, to the best of his knowledge, he had not.

Salmons then asked the Sheriff if it were not true all the streetlights had been broken in front and around the jail on the night of violence. The big lawman answered in the affirmative as the defense attorney stood near the jury box, seemingly pondering the answer to his question.

Salmons then walked back across the front of the courtroom and stood very near the witness. Then, fixing his eyes upon the Sheriff, he demanded to know how Whitlock could identify a man he had never seen before, on a dark night, in a large crowd while he, Whitlock, stood on a brightly lit porch.

Whitlock was unshaken by the attorney's courtroom manner. His voice remained strong and sure as he pointed out Baker had been but a short distance from him when he had fired his gun. He had been clearly illuminated by the lights on the porch of the jail. He related again the Kentuckian had approached the jail and had been only a few feet from him when he told the Sheriff if he did not get the prisoners, someone would be killed. Whitlock said he had no doubt Baker was the man who had attempted to kill him.

Deputy Runyan was then called to the stand and promptly identified Baker as the man who had attempted to kill the Sheriff. The defendant seemed unconcerned by the testimony being given against him as he sat quietly watching the proceedings. Runyan testified he had observed the Kentuckian, with a revolver in each hand, swearing at the Sheriff and calling upon the mob to lynch the lawman. He further stated he saw Baker shoot at the Sheriff from only a short distance away. On cross examination the deputy maintained his composure and his testimony was unshaken.

Deputy Newlin, Doctor Sims, and Constable VanVickle all took turns on the witness stand and each identified Baker as one of those at the jail taking part in the riot. The men testified they had heard him making threats against the prisoners and the lawmen, and they had seen him throw stones at the jail building. Deputy Newlin had also observed the defendant shooting at the jail.

When the lanky defendant took his turn on the witness stand, he seemed as self assured as had those who appeared against him. Though Baker had initially told the judge he would defend himself, he had decided he needed a "real" attorney for his defense. He denied all the charges that had been made against him. Baker admitted he had been in Danville on the night of the riot, having come to the city in the early evening in a rig. The tall, farm laborer related he had only been in Vermilion County a few months and he had been employed during his time in the county. On the night of the riot he said he had left his horse and rig at the livery just across the street from the county jail.

Baker was mixed up as to the points of the compass and it took Attorney Salmons, much to the amusement of some of the onlookers, some time to get the farmhand located as to the proper directions.

Once Baker had his directions straight, he testified after he had made arrangements for his rig, he walked north on Vermilion Street, away from the jail. When he reached Main Street, he met a friend of his, Thomas Blakeslee, in front of the saloon by Fera's Grocery.

The Kentuckian calmly testified he never spoke to the Sheriff or any of his deputies on the night of the riot. In fact, he said, at the time the attack on the jail took place, he was in Depke's Saloon.

Baker testified he had left the city about 10:30 P M. He had seen the body of the Negro, Metcalf, burning when he left town. He also reported he had seen the rail on the front steps of the jail building, but, he maintained, he did not take any part in the riot and he was not present in the mob at the jail. He further stated he was not carrying any weapons on the night of the riot, though he admitted he was armed when he was arrested. When Salmons asked Baker how long he was in town on the night the riot took place the Kentuckian responded he was in Danville about an hour and a half.

When State's Attorney Keeslar cross-examined the Kentuckian he was unable to shake his testimony. He thought he had Baker trapped on the Kentuckian's statement that he had been in Depke's Saloon at the time of the riot. Keeslar was well aware that all saloons had been ordered closed at 10:00 P.M. A deputy was sent to question Depke as to what time he closed on the night of the riot. The lawman returned and informed the prosecutor the saloon was open well past the ordered closing time. Keeslar appeared to be the only one surprised by the news, as many of the spectators in the courtroom exchanged knowing glances. Baker was excused from the witness stand and the name Thomas Blakeslee was called.

Blakeslee was a man who appeared to be in his late twenties or early thirties. He was extremely nervous as he was sworn in. Defense attorney Salmons asked the witness how long he had known the defendant. Blakeslee answered he had known Baker for a number of months. Salmons then asked the witness a series of questions in an effort to establish an alibi for Baker during the time the violence took place at the county jail.

Blakeslee testified he had met the defendant near Fera's Grocery on West Main in Danville on the night of the riot. He remembered they had talked for a short time, then he had left Baker to go pick up Mrs. Blakeslee at Shepards' Restaurant. The witness testified when he left Baker, he was standing in front of the Palmer Bank on Main Street.

It only took Blakeslee a few minutes to walk to the restaurant, which was located on East Main Street. He testified that when he reached the eatery, he was unable to locate his wife so he returned to where he had left Baker. He found the Kentuckian still standing on the corner by the bank. Blakeslee estimated he spent about ten minutes looking for his wife. The witness then said he and Baker decided to walk down to the jail and the two of them headed in that direction. But before they reached the scene of the rioting, they changed their minds and reversed directions and walked back north on Vermilion Street. Blakeslee reported he left Baker at the old Goldsmith corner while he once again went in search of his wife.

When Salmons finished with his questions, he took his seat next to Baker. State's Attorney Keeslar stood and walked to the front of the courtroom. The witness appeared to be more nervous than ever as the prosecutor approached him to begin the cross-examination. Keeslar asked the man if he had ever found his wife. Blakeslee answered that he had, and when he found her, she was having a conversation with defendant Baker. The attorney then asked the man what time it was when he found his wife conversing with Baker. Blakeslee answered it was about 11:00 P.M. when he found the two of them talking at the corner of South and Hazel Streets. Keeslar noted this was a half hour after the time Baker had testified he had left the city. He then asked Blakeslee, who was now fidgeting in his chair, how long his wife had been talking to the Kentuckian. The witness testified that his wife had told him she and Baker had been together about forty-five minutes. When Keeslar asked Blakeslee how long he was separated from Baker during the evening, the man could not remember for sure. The state's attorney then asked the witness if he, at anytime, had gone near the rioters in the downtown area. Blakeslee swore he never had. Keeslar noted that was "very curious" and then took his seat and the court called the next witness for the defense.

Jay Phillips took the stand and almost at once proved an excellent witness for the prosecution, though he had been called by the defense. Phillips testified Baker had the reputation of being a peaceable citizen in the neighborhood where they lived. He then told the defense attorney Baker had picked him and his wife up about 1:00 A.M. Sunday morning near the Children's Home and had given them a ride to their home. This was an hour and a half after the time the defendant testified he had left the city. Defense attorney Salmons attempted to have this testimony stricken from the record, but it was left standing.

Keeslar did not subject Phillips to a severe cross-examination, but he did question him as to the time when the Kentuckian had picked him and his wife up. The witness once again testified it was 1:00 A.M. when Baker had given them a ride. Keeslar then walked over to the jury and noted this was in direct conflict with the testimony given by the defendant.

It was growing late in the afternoon and it was clear to everyone in the courtroom that things were not going in defendant Baker's favor. A number of character witnesses had taken the stand to testify for the Kentuckian, but one of these, under cross-examination, had admitted his father had suggested he not associate with Baker.

At this time one of the defense attorneys took the stand in behalf of their defendant. This caused a stirring in the crowd of onlookers, and a number of men took the opportunity to use the spittoons that were placed in strategic places in the courtroom. The stained floor around the vessels gave evidence of why storekeepers posted signs instructing the tobacco chewers to "spit on each other, not the floor."

Attorney Earl Brown was the picture of confidence as he looked out at the packed courtroom from the witness chair. As his co-council for the defense, George Salmons questioned him, he answered in a firm, convincing voice.

Brown testified he had been at the county jail on the night of the riot, observing the violence. He said he was standing just a little north and east of the jail at about 10:00 P.M. in the evening. He remarked he was only about fifteen feet from where the Sheriff and the other witnesses had said Baker stood and fired. When this testimony came out, the courtroom became silent as the witness had captured everyone's attention. Even State's Attorney Keeslar ceased the gentle drumming of his fingers on the prosecutor's table.

Brown reported he had seen the man fire the shots and it was not Baker. He testified the assailant was a head shorter than Baker and that while his clothes were not dark, they certainly were not white. He further testified he had not observed Baker in the group of rioters on the night of violence.

As soon as Brown had given his testimony, he made a move to leave the witness chair, but Keeslar at once called out he was going to cross-examine.

Brown was a large man and he made an imposing figure in the witness chair. But as the prosecuting attorney approached the defense lawyer, it was clear to the observers Brown was not happy at being the subject of a cross- examination.

Keeslar meticulously began to go over Brown's testimony, asking the same questions Salmons had asked. Brown became argumentative when Keeslar asked how he could see a man in a packed crowd if he were some distance away and unusually short. Judge Thompson advised Brown he was in the witness chair and he would have to answer the questions. But it was becoming clear to the onlookers, the witness, who had appeared to be so professional, was now struggling. Keeslar then moved from where he had been standing near his chair to the front of the courtroom. The small prosecutor then turned and faced the jury, but he directed his question to the man in the witness chair. He asked that if the clothes the man who fired the shots was wearing were not dark and they were not light, what color were they? This question proved to be the final straw for Brown. He erupted in a tirade that brought Judge Thompson's gavel pounding on his podium. The judge warned the witness he was an attorney and he knew how a witness should conduct himself when on the stand. He then told Brown to answer the questions put to him direct, and to refrain from making any further comments. Brown reluctantly admitted that Baker might have fired at Sheriff Whitlock without him knowing it. Keeslar showed a hint of a smile as he drew this bit of testimony from the opposing attorney. He took his seat and Attorney Brown did the same.

It was now late in the day and Judge Thompson asked the attorneys to approach the bench. The last witness had been heard. He asked the lawyers if they wanted to make their final arguments. Keeslar was ready to continue, but Salmons said the defense would not have enough time to make their arguments at the late hour. Thompson then adjourned the trial until the next day.

Winfield Baker was escorted back to the county jail by Sheriff Whitlock and three deputies. As the men made their way through the crowd that was milling around the courthouse following the trial, a number of people called out encouragement to the cheerful Baker. The Kentuckian, reported one of the deputies, was as "peaceable as he would have been had he just been to a church picnic." The trip between the courthouse and the jail only took a few minutes but the way was lined with the curious as well as a few friends of Baker. The crowds would grow larger as the court appearances of the accused continued.

August 25th found Whitlock once again visited by two "fine citizens." The men were accompanied by, but not supported by, Colonel Buckingham. The trio met with the lawman at an early hour of the morning as the trial would commence in the early forenoon. The mission of the "citizens" was the same as that of the many who had come before them. The Sheriff was told it would be in his best interests as well as the city's to "find a way out" for the others accused, once Baker was convicted, as it appeared he would be. As the Sheriff silently listened to the men, he was urged to "talk to" Keeslar and bring the riot proceedings to a conclusion. One of the men informed Whitlock that this was more a matter of "race, than of law," and the lawman "had better get on the right side."

The Sheriff informed the visitors that in the sight of the law, it was not a matter of race, but a matter of justice. He told the "citizens" he had stood his ground when threatened by scores of rioters on the night of the lynching and he certainly was not going to be "buffaloed" by their threats. Whitlock then ushered the men out of the jail, as the pair continued to inform him he "did not know what was good for him."

At 9:00 A.M. the jury was ready to hear the final arguments in the Baker trial. Keeslar had been informed of the visit the Sheriff had received early in the morning from the "fine citizens." The only effect it seemed to have on the slender attorney was to further motivate him.

Attorney Salmons made an earnest appeal for a verdict of innocence for his client. He argued there was little evidence against the accused man and Baker had established an alibi for the time he was reportedly at the jail. The lawyer remarked Baker was a hard working, well liked member of the community. To participate in a riot, or to make an assault on the Sheriff, was not in the man's nature. Salmon's closing statement was brief despite his request for additional time.

State's Attorney Keeslar pointed out Baker's own witnesses gave testimony directly in conflict with the story of the defendant. As the prosecutor walked slowly to the front of the jury box, he noted it was indeed curious that Baker had not gone to the jail when "nearly everyone" in the city seemed to have been drawn to the scene of violence. He shot a look at defense attorney Brown who had earlier testified he had gone to the jail as an "observer" during the riot. The attorney then told the jury Baker had not only gone to the jail, but he had also been a leader in all that had happened on the night of violence. He called for a verdict of guilty as the only just verdict available.

Judge Thompson instructed the jury in its duties and the jury retired to render a decision. Sheriff Whitlock and his deputies escorted Baker back to his cell in the county jail to wait on the decision of the jury. Many of the trial watchers and the reporters covering the event stayed in the courthouse. Seats were going at a premium and the observers were reluctant to lose their places in an event which was becoming a historic happening.

While the jury was deliberating the case, Harmon Manigold, a house painter from Danville, walked to the south doorway of the courthouse and began denouncing Sheriff Whitlock for arresting and bringing the rioters to trial. Manigold had a strong voice and it rolled across the brick paved city square. It only took moments for the man to assemble a small audience of sympathetic listeners. As the crowd grew in numbers, Manigold's voice rose to a hoarse shout as he told the assemblage what should be done with a man like Whitlock. He told his listeners when a man was taken out of a livery stable and put on horseback as sheriff, it might be expected he would ride the horse to death.

Heads nodded in agreement and shouts of encouragement rang out from those gathered around the house painter. The crowd was now backed up into the street and growing by the second. Manigold told the people the Sheriff should have been thankful there were citizens, good law abiding citizens, willing to do a job he could not or would not do. He shouted it was a disgrace a lot of good men were sitting in jail for attempting to carry out the law.

As soon as Manigold had began his tirade against Whitlock, word had been sent to the jail there was potential trouble developing at the courthouse. There were hundreds of men in the downtown area, many of them laid off miners who were on hand to see the outcome of the trial. All it would take was one spark to touch off another round of violence in the city on the Vermilion.

Manigold's speech had become quite rabid by the time deputies and troops were dispatched to the courthouse. He told the crowd he had voted for Whitlock because he was a poor man, but now he was willing to spend a thousand dollars to get rid of him. At this point, Deputy Newlin arrived on the scene. The stocky lawman pushed his way through the excited onlookers and grabbed Manigold by the shirt and yanked him from the doorway of the courthouse. Armed soldiers scattered the gathering of men and took up positions near the building to discourage any further activity.

Newlin led the now bewildered Manigold away from the courthouse to the jail. Manigold, who was intoxicated, informed the deputy it was the liquor that had caused him to speak out. He also commented he had heard some of the lawmen make disparaging remarks about the rioters, and he had taken offense at what he had heard. As Newlin pushed and pulled his reluctant prisoner to the county jail on South Vermilion Street, he was aware many of the men they were passing were as intoxicated as Manigold.

Manigold was charged with inciting a riot, and when he could produce no money for bail, he was given lodging in the county jail with the prisoners he had been so loudly sympathetic about. Whitlock had just finished settling his newest customer when word came the jury was coming in with a verdict and he was to bring Baker back to the courthouse.

The jury had only been out about an hour and some of the press people were surprised by the swiftness of their decision. When all the principals were back in the courtroom, foreman of the jury L.M. Erickson turned in the verdict. The lanky Kentuckian showed no emotion as the verdict of guilty as charged was read. He told those within hearing he had wanted to plead guilty when arrested, but his attorneys had talked him out of it. As Baker was led from the courtroom, he knew he faced a prison sentence, but he confided to one of the onlookers he would "have plenty of company."

Chapter Twenty

Judge Thompson spent the rest of August 25th in search of a jury to decide the fate of those who would be tried next. They would be Winfield Baker (again), John (Jack) Walton, Adam Murray, Isaac Newton Slade, John Robertson, Thomas Bell, Clay Biddle, and William Redwine. These men were charged with inciting to riot. If convicted, the men would face a jail term or probation, not a prison sentence.

The judge now discovered people were unwilling to serve on a jury to decide the fate of the accused rioters. He had filled the jury box with little trouble for the Baker trial, but that was not going to happen again. As prospective juror after juror was dismissed for various reasons, it became apparent the judge's patience was wearing thin. Man after man informed the court they had reached an unshakable decision as to the innocence or guilt of the accused and their decisions would not be changed. Dozens of men passed before the court as the afternoon wore into evening; the names in the box of prospective jurors was dwindling rapidly.

One man, in particular, irritated Thompson. He informed the judge although he did not know the defendants, knew nothing about their connection with the riot, he did know he had a fixed opinion as to their guilt or innocence. Thompson told the man he had no right to such an opinion if he did not have knowledge of the events and people involved. The prospective juror maintained he certainly did have such a right and his mind would not be changed. After giving the reluctant juror a lecture on the responsibilities of citizens in a free society, the judge dismissed him, much to the amusement of the people in the packed courtroom.

By late evening, all the individuals whose names had been placed in the box as possible jurors had been dismissed and there were no more names to call. Keeslar told Whitlock they might not have to worry about a prejudiced jury, it appeared no one was willing to serve. There were now empty seats in the courtroom as many of the trial watchers had left for their suppers or to visit the downtown saloons, which were just beginning to do a lively business. Only the reporters stayed at their posts, reluctant to miss anything that might happen.

Judge Thompson now had men brought in off the street as potential jurors. The press was treated to another humorous incident when one of the men brought in thought he was being arrested. By the time the jury was filled to hear the next trial, streetlights were casting their radiance about the courthouse and the sun had long since disappeared on the western horizon. The second trial for the rioters of 1903 would begin in the morning.

The night of August 25th was not to be uneventful. A fight among three black women at the intersection of Washington and Main Streets drew the attention of Officer Leverenz. When the policeman tried to break up the disturbance, one of the women attacked him. Before the fracas ended Leverenz and two of the women had been injured. Patrolman Flynn, who was working nearby, came to Leverenz's aid and assisted in taking one of the women to police headquarters. The husband of the woman arrested followed the two policemen and his wife.

Word of the disturbance spread quickly and a crowd of about a hundred men quickly gathered about the city building where the woman was taken. When the husband began to complain about his wife's arrest, the men made a move to detain the man and he escaped by running away. The men chased after him for a short distance, but lost him in the darkness of the August night. The soldiers were alerted but there was no further trouble.

The city police criticized the sheriff's deputies for not assisting Officer Leverenz. Two deputies had reportedly responded when they heard of the trouble but were said to have done nothing to help Leverenz, who nearly had his thumb severed in the fight.

On the morning of August 26th, Whitlock and his deputies escorted eight prisoners from the county jail on South Vermilion Street to the courthouse. As had happened before, a large number of friends and supporters of the accused men lined the sidewalk to watch the lawmen and their charges pass. Many in the crowd called out to the handcuffed men as they were led up the street. Jack Walton was particularly popular with the crowd, and he exchanged a few good natured remarks with those who called out. Following the Manigold incident of the previous day, the military men were in a heightened state of readiness.

The courthouse was so full that Whitlock and his deputies had to clear a path to move the defendants to the courtroom. As the prisoners were ushered to their seats, many in the crowded courtroom seemed to regard them more as celebrities than as accused criminals. Once they were all seated and the Sheriff and his deputies had taken seats behind them, Judge Thompson entered the room.

Thompson pounded his gavel and sternly called for quiet. It took several moments for the room full of people to lower their voices to what the judge regarded as an acceptable level. He had already informed the attorneys on both sides he would not allow the trial to be turned into a circus. He had also warned the press about printing inflammatory half-truths about the proceedings. Now the judge reminded everyone in his courtroom they were at a legal proceeding and they would be expected to conduct themselves in the appropriate manner.

Sheriff Whitlock was called to the stand, as in the trial with Baker, he would be the main witness for the prosecution. The big lawman identified each of the defendants and explained what he had witnessed them doing on the night of the riot. Only young Clay Biddle seemed concerned as the Sheriff pointed to each of the men in the prisoners' dock. When Keeslar had finished with Whitlock, Attorney Salmons moved to the front of the courtroom to question the lawman.

Salmons was an experienced trial attorney, he had been practicing law since 1876. He had failed to shake Whitlock's testimony on the previous day and now the lawman had delivered the same damaging testimony. Salmons had been criticized for not pushing Whitlock harder. One of the other attorneys had informed him Whitlock was just a "big, uneducated stable boy," and he would crack under a tough cross-examination. Salmons had reminded the other lawyer, since Whitlock did not "crack" when there were a thousand men storming his jail, it was highly unlikely that he would do so now. Salmons did not look down on what some considered Whitlock's humble beginnings. He himself had worked his way to a law degree as a farm laborer and school teacher.

The defense attorney once again asked Whitlock how he could be sure of the identity of the rioters since all the streetlights had been broken. The lawman again informed Salmons that the electric lights on the porch of the jail allowed him to see faces in the mob. He added, there were a number of torches and lanterns being carried by some of the people on the street. He also mentioned the straw and railroad tie fire that had been built about the body of Metcalf blazed brightly at times. Whitlock also pointed out some light came from the windows of the jail.

Salmons saw he was making little progress with the light issue so he changed his tact. He slowly walked to the jury box and then turned to face Whitlock. He then asked the Sheriff how far the shot from his riot gun would carry. Whitlock answered he was not an expert on firearms and would not be able to give an accurate estimate. Salmons then rephrased his question and asked if the gun would not carry a hundred yards. This caused a brief stirring in the courtroom, as there were few men present who did not know something about shooting a shotgun. Whitlock showed he did have some knowledge of firearms when he answered he doubted the shot would carry effectively that far. Salmons was trying to make it appear the rioters were some distance from the jail when they were shot, but his questioning had the opposite effect. Those with any knowledge at all of a riot gun knew, for it to be very effective, the targets had to be at close range. Salmons then took his seat and Whitlock was excused. Those watching reported Whitlock had bested Salmons.

The last witness to be called before the noon hour was Attorney Samuel F. Schecter. Though he hadn't been admitted to the bar yet, Schecter was studying law and referred to himself as an attorney. When Prosecutor Keeslar asked the witness where he was on the night of the riot, Schecter replied he had gone to the area of the jail to watch the excitement, carefully adding he had not been a participant. This brought snickers from the crowded courtroom and a call for quiet from Thompson.

Schecter testified he had seen Jack Walton help attack the jail, and he had heard Isaac Slade going through the mob asking the women and children to leave. When Keeslar asked why Slade was asking the women and children to move away from the jail, the witness said it was because the jail was to be blown up. This caused another stir in the courtroom and yet another call for silence from Thompson. Keeslar took his seat and began to drum his fingers lightly on the small table holding his papers.

Attorney Brown now got to his feet to cross-examine the witness. He walked to the front of the room and then asked Schecter, in a loud voice, what he was really doing at the jail during the riot. Before he could answer, Keeslar was objecting to the question and Thompson sustained the objection. It seemed a strange question to some of those present because Brown himself had admitted on the previous day he had been on the street in front of the jail at the time of the riot.

Brown then asked the witness to describe exactly where he was when he observed the two men he had named in his testimony. At this point Schecter began to struggle and became mixed up in his testimony. He admitted he could not be positive he had observed Slade, but he was almost certain he had seen Jack Walton. Brown was smiling as he walked back to where the defendants were seated and Attorney Schecter seemed very relieved to be out of the witness chair. On this note Thompson adjourned the trial for lunch.

During the noon recess Judge Thompson had a brief meeting with the attorneys involved in the trial. He told them if the public continued to disrupt the proceedings he would bar them from the courtroom. He pointedly told the defense attorneys the trial would be decided by a jury, not by public opinion. He noted a decision must be based on facts, not on friendships, politics, and half truths. He told the small group this was serious business, no one should take the crimes committed lightly. A man had been lynched, burned, and butchered on the streets of Danville. Officers of the law had been assailed and injured, public and private property had been destroyed. When the judge dismissed the attorneys, one of the defense lawyers commented he sounded more like a prosecutor than a sitting judge.

When the court was called to order for the afternoon session, Deputy Runyan was called to the stand in the hot courtroom. Prosecutor Keeslar stood near the line of defendants sitting with their attorneys. He then asked the lawman if he could identify any of the men. Runyan identified each of the eight accused and testified he had seen them taking part in the violence at the jail. He reported he had clearly seen Slade running around crying he had been shot, after the shots were fired on the south side of the jail. Attorney Brown objected to this, arguing that because a man had been shot it should not be assumed he was involved in the riot. Thompson overruled the objection and the testimony stood. Runyan also testified that Clay Biddle was throwing rocks from the market house at the jail. Keeslar then took his seat and Salmons made his way to the front of the room and confronted Runyan.

He asked the deputy where he was on the night of the riot. This brought laughter from the courtroom because it was well known that Runyan had been in the thick of things on the night of violence. He calmly told the defense attorney he had been at the jail. Then Salmons told him he wanted to know where he was, exactly, when he witnessed all the men he had testified against. Runyan paused for a few moments and soon after gave a brief description of his movements on the night of the riot. He remembered Winfield Baker in particular because, he told the attorney, Baker had informed him they were going to "hang some more niggers" before the night was over. Salmons at once asked for this testimony to be struck from the record, as no one was on trial for hanging anyone. Thompson agreed and the jurors were told to disregard the "hanging" remark. After this exchange, Salmons ended his cross-examination. The defense lawyers had been careful to keep any reference to the lynching of John Metcalf out of the courtroom testimony.

The afternoon was taken up with a number of witnesses called by Prosecutor Keeslar to testify. Noah Jones and Charles Lloyd both had a turn on the stand and identified William Redwine as being the man who had told them he had taken part in the riot. Both men said Redwine had told of having hold of the rail when Whitlock had fired his gun down it. They said the defendant informed them he was wounded by the blast.

It was late in the afternoon when Judge Thompson recessed the trial until the next morning. Following his noon session with the attorneys, the courtroom had been more orderly. Thompson's threat to clear the courtroom had evidently paid off.

Once again the sheriff and his deputies moved the prisoners back to the county jail, which was now called Hotel Whitlock by some of the defendants' friends. A number of the men who had been on hand in the courtroom went straight to Depke's Saloon to give the details of the trial to those who had not been fortunate enough to attend. As the buckets of beer flowed to the thirsty customers, they lamented the fate of their comrades languishing in the county jail.

August 27th saw the trial continue with more prosecution witnesses lined up to appear. The first man to be called by State's Attorney Keeslar was Constable Fred Jahuke. The Constable testified he had been in front of the jail on the night of the violence and had witnessed Winfield Baker taking part in the riot. He said the Kentuckian had a revolver in each hand and when asked what he was going to do with the weapons he replied, "We are going to get into this jail and get some of those fellows."

Justice of the Peace Allen Grant was sworn in and testified he had been standing on the south side of the jail on the night of the riot. Grant reported he heard a shot that "sounded like a cannon" and saw a man grab his head and shout "My God, I am shot!" On cross-examination Justice Grant said he could not be sure the man shot was Adam Murray.

The last witness called by the prosecution was Doctor John M. Guy. Keeslar asked the physician to identify the men he had treated on the night of the riot. Guy pointed out Adam Murray and Thomas Bell. He explained that Bell was wounded by buckshot, but it appeared to him, Murray had been shot with a solid bullet. This caused a stirring in the courtroom, as it had been assumed the Sheriff did all the shooting with his riot gun.

When the state had finished with their witnesses, the first of the defendants, Adam Murray, was called to the stand by defense attorney Dennis. The twenty-seven year old Dennis was one of the youngest attorneys involved in the trial. But his performance in the courtroom exhibited the skill which would eventually take him to the state legislature and to the attorney general's office in Springfield. As the dark haired, youthful appearing attorney waited for Murray to be sworn in, he smiled pleasantly at the jurors. Murray was a man who appeared to be about thirty years of age and he seemed to be well composed as he swore to tell the truth.

When Dennis asked the witness to describe his activities on the night of July 25th, he was taken aback by the man's first statement. Murray said, "In the first place, my name is Adam Merry not Adam

Murray, it always has been Merry and always will be." This brought laughter from the onlookers and a smile to Judge Thompson's face, which contrasted sharply with the stern look he usually presented in the courtroom. Murray carefully spelled his name and requested it be changed on all the court records. He was told it would be. (It wasn't).

Murray then testified he had gone to the jail about 9:30 in the evening to watch the crowd. He reported he spent most of his time on the south side of the jail, just watching the others. Murray noted the light was so dim it was impossible to "see anyone." He said he did not take any part in the "proceedings." He denied he had ever shouted for the rioters to attack the jail. He also testified he never waved his arms in a threatening motion. He said the only time he raised his voice was when he called on the mob to be quiet and give the Sheriff a chance to speak. Murray further testified he had been standing at the south side of the jail, not saying a word, his hands folded behind him, when he had been shot. He said the blood from the wound blinded him but he did not fall or cry out. He walked to the livery stable and was taken to the hospital in an ambulance.

A.B. Dennis turned the witness over to Keeslar to be cross-examined and took his seat with the other defendants and attorneys.

Keeslar asked Murray if he had seen anyone he knew in the mob on the night of the violence. Murray replied in the negative, once again repeating the light was too "dim" to see anyone. Then Keeslar asked where he was, exactly, when the attacks were made on the jail. Murray replied he had been across the street at the fire, watching Metcalf burn. Once again the state's attorney repeated the first question, asking "in all those hundreds of people, was there not one" that Murray could identify?

The witness hesitated a few seconds, and then said he did remember seeing Andy Baker and Jack Hall in the crowd. He further testified he had seen Isaac Newton Slade and Harry Rennick, but, he added, they were taking no part in the rioting. Now Keeslar asked at what distance he had been from the men when he saw them. Murray answered he "guessed" he was about twenty feet away. Keeslar then asked Murray if he had ever spent any time in prison. The defendant hesitated a few moments and then said as a matter of fact he had. He admitted he had been sentenced to thirteen months in the penitentiary in 1895 for stealing a bicycle.

Keeslar told the judge he had no further questions and took his seat. He had established the fact there was enough light for the men to be identified in the mob. He had also placed Murray's prison record before the jury.

Attorney Dennis requested all the testimony of Murray, in regard to Slade, be excluded from the record. Judge Thompson denied his motion. Dennis appeared upset by the judge's decision, he looked as if he were going to say more but thought better of it and moved on to the next witness.

Andy Brown, a young man from Grape Creek, Illinois, took the stand next. Brown appeared to be extremely nervous as Dennis led him through his testimony. He told the court he had been in town on the night of the riot, just walking around through the large crowd. He testified he had seen Adam Murray there and the miner was taking no part in the violence. He reported Murray, too, was just peaceably walking about. At no time did the young miner see Murray do anything unlawful. Dennis then took his seat and turned the witness over to Keeslar.

The prosecutor walked to the front of the room and stood beside Brown. Then, in a friendly tone, he asked the witness if he was acquainted with Lon VanCamp who also lived in Grape Creek. The young man answered in the affirmative. Keeslar then began to walk slowly across the front of the courtroom and asked Brown if he had seen the body of Metcalf burning on the straw fire across from the county jail. Brown admitted he had seen the lynching victim's body on top of the fire. Then the state's attorney turned on the witness, all his friendliness gone. "And isn't it true," he demanded "that you told Lon VanCamp you piled straw on the burning body of the murdered man?"

Dennis was on his feet objecting to the question, but before Thompson could rule, Brown said he could not remember telling such a story. The judge let the question stand and Keeslar ended his cross-examination. A very relieved Andy Brown made his way to the back of the courtroom.

Harry Rennick, a smooth faced teenager who lived in Catlin, Illinois, was next called to the stand. Rennick had been indicted on another count but was not yet on trial. The youth appeared to be terrified as he was sworn in and he kept his eyes on the floor. George Salmons approached the witness and told him not to be nervous, to just tell the truth.

Attorney Salmons then asked Rennick where he was on the night of the incident at the jail. The youth answered, in a barely audible voice, he had been in front of the jail. He said he had been drawn there by all the noise the mob was making. Salmons asked if he had seen anyone he knew at the jail. Rennick answered he had seen Adam Murray near the jail, but Murray had been doing nothing, just watching the others.

After Salmons took his seat, Keeslar briefly cross-examined the young witness. It appeared even Keeslar was sympathetic to the obviously frightened youth as he questioned him. He asked Rennick a number of questions, establishing where he was on the night of violence. Then in a quiet voice he asked the witness how he was able to identify Murray in the darkness of the night. To this Rennick answered there was enough light to "see people." Then Keeslar asked him how close he had been to Murray when he identified him. The youth answered he had been "some little distance" from the miner when he had seen him. After drawing this answer, a satisfied Keeslar took his seat.

Mary Brigham was then called to the stand as a witness for the defense. As the young woman in the long dress made her way to the witness stand, the courtroom became noticeably quieter. Brigham appeared composed and self-assured as she swore to tell the truth. Salmons asked her if she had seen Clay Biddle on the night of the riot. The woman answered "yes" in a strong voice, contrasting sharply with the two preceding witnesses.

The resident of 215 Green Street testified she and her husband had heard the noise of the rioters and had gone to the corner of College and Main Streets to watch the excitement. It was at this point they met Clay Biddle. She estimated the time to be about 7:30 in the evening. They watched the crowds at the intersection for a time and then, when the crowd moved away, they went to the South Street crossing of the Wabash Railroad and watched the rioters from there. They watched the rioting from this location until about 10:30 P.M. and then decided to go home. Brigham testified she walked Biddle home because she wanted to visit a relative who lived near him. Salmons took his seat and Keeslar moved to the front of the jury to cross-examine.

Keeslar asked Brigham where she was standing when she was at the College and Main Streets intersection. The woman answered she had been standing on the "south side" of Main Street. Then the prosecutor asked if she had observed the lynching of Metcalf, which had occurred less than half a block away. Before she could answer, a course of objections were raised from the row of attorneys seated with the defendants. Keeslar withdrew the question before Thompson could rule, then he walked very near the witness chair.

He asked the witness why she left the intersection to go to the South Street location. Brigham answered she left because the crowd had all moved after the body of Metcalf had been dragged past the corner. The defense attorneys once again objected to Keeslar's line of questioning, but this time they were overruled by Thompson.

As the slender state's attorney continued to question the young woman, some of her earlier confidence seemed to disappear. When Keeslar asked her a second time what time it was she first met Biddle, she replied she did not know for sure. He then asked her if the young man had been with her all the time after she first met him. The witness was silent a few moments and then admitted Biddle was not with her all the time. At times, she testified, he would disappear into the mob. But, she added in a lower voice, he always returned. Keeslar walked to his chair and announced he was finished with the witness.

The time was nearing the noon hour and Thompson recessed the trial. Once again many of the spectators in the room kept their seats so they would not lose them when the trial resumed. As Whitlock and his men moved the prisoners out of the courtroom for the return trip to the jail, the Sheriff was treated to a few caustic remarks from friends of the accused.

The afternoon session saw more witnesses called to testify to the innocence of those on trial. The theme of the testimony was the same. The people on the witness stand had observed the indicted men in the mob and they had been doing nothing. Keeslar did not cross-examine every person called to the stand by the defense. He sat quietly watching, his fingers tapping lightly on the table holding his papers. He would occasionally voice an objection which was usually upheld by Judge Thompson. One of the defense lawyers noted later, in his opinion, the judge acted as co-council for the prosecution.

Doctor French was called to the stand and he testified he had treated the wound on Clay Biddle's knee. The physician reported, in his opinion, the wound had not been caused by a gunshot. When Keeslar cross-examined the doctor, the medical man could not remember which knee it was he had treated on the boy. When asked if he was the Biddle family physician, he stated he was not.

Biddle was then called to the stand and A.B. Dennis led him through his testimony. Biddle reported he had not been at the jail at all on the night of the riot. He testified he had hurt his knee when he had been pushed to the ground by the mob on East Main Street. He further stated he had been merely joking when he told people he had been shot by the Sheriff.

When Keeslar came forward to cross-examine the youth, there was a stirring in the courtroom. A number of Biddle's family members and friends were present and Thompson had to call for quiet as the state's attorney asked his first question.

Keeslar asked Biddle if he told Deputy Runyan he had been injured at city hall when Metcalf was being taken from that building. The youth denied he had told such a story. The prosecutor then asked if he had been present at the lynching of the Negro. Defense Attorney Dennis objected to this question and the objection was sustained by Thompson. The state's attorney then asked if it were not true that he had told Juergens, Lemon, and Spencer he had been shot while attacking the county jail. The young man admitted he had told Juergens such a story, but he had only been joking. He denied telling Lemon and Spencer he had been shot. He had only told them he had been hurt by the rioters.

Keeslar then asked the boy where he was from. Biddle testified he was from Parke County, Indiana, and his parents still resided there. When asked when he moved to Vermilion County, the youth became confused and it was clear to those watching he did not understand the months of the year. He testified he first came to the county in September. When Keeslar pointed out September had not yet arrived, the witness said it "must have been" February.

At this point Biddle's mother jumped to her feet in the audience and shouted February was not the month he had come to the county. Keeslar told the woman to shut up, her son was testifying. Thompson banged his gavel and brought the courtroom back to order as two of the deputies stood and walked to the back of the room. Biddle's mother sat down as the two lawmen approached and the tense moment passed.

Keeslar now asked Biddle, if it were not true, that he had left Indiana because a warrant had been issued for him in that state. The defense objected, but before the judge could rule, the youth answered it was not true. Keeslar then took his seat and Biddle was dismissed.

Attorney William Beckwith walked to the front of the courtroom to question Jack Walton. Beckwith was an imposing figure as he stood before the court. He was of medium height with very wide shoulders. A well trimmed beard hid his lower face, but his dark eyes were intense as he slowly viewed the jury members before he began his questioning.

Jack Walton wore a smile as he waited for Beckwith to begin his questioning. The miner was a man in his mid-thirties and his smile was returned by many of those sitting in the crowded room. It was clear the affable Walton was the most popular defendant in the courtroom.

Beckwith asked the witness to describe his activities on the night of the riot. Walton said he could remember very little of what happened on the night of July 25th. He recollected, much to the amusement of those in the court, he had started drinking very early on that day and by night he was drunk. He had no memory of the lynching, the riot, or anything else which had happened on the night of July 25th. He was positive if he was at the jail, pointing out he had no memory of his whereabouts, he would have been too drunk to have taken any part in the attack. His first memory of the riot was on the following morning, July 26th, when one of his friends told him about it. He remembered, quite clearly, telling the friend the Sheriff "did the right thing" by shooting into the mob. Keeslar objected to this statement and the judge ruled it out.

Keeslar did not cross-examine Walton, noting later he thought "Jack was one of the few of the defendants who actually told the truth."

The trial was adjourned at 5:00 P.M. and the closing arguments would be heard the next day. As the defense attorneys left the room, one of them noted the judge was leaning strongly toward the prosecution. Though the defendants would not go to prison if convicted in this trial, the attorneys realized the same evidence would be heard in the "big trial" which was to follow. If the accused were found guilty in the current court proceedings, it would have an impact on the next case.

Attorney Dennis noted one of the goals of the defense had been to keep any mention of the lynching of Metcalf out of the courtroom. But "he (Keeslar) managed to resurrect the Negro for nearly every witness. Even though no one was being tried for what happened to him, the jury was reminded over and over of the lynching and burning of the man."

Chapter Twenty-one

On the morning of August 28th, eleven jurors gathered to hear the final arguments in the trial. The twelfth juror, C. F. Clayton, had been dismissed when his wife suddenly became ill. Both sides had agreed to continue with eleven jurors.

The five defense attorneys were told by Thompson they could have two and a half hours to make their statements. The prosecution was given an hour and a half. Keeslar appealed for more time but Thompson told him an hour and a half would be sufficient.

The courtroom was packed once again. The spectators crowded each other closer together on the polished benches as they waited for the trial to begin. Judge Thompson surveyed the scene from his small island of justice and banged his gavel down. The noise in the room fell to a few whispering voices in the back. The attorneys began their arguments.

The defense built its case around the claim the defendants were merely innocent bystanders on the night of the riot. They contended the fact some of them had been shot was just an unfortunate accident and should not be considered an indication of guilt.

Attorney Chambers pointed out Clay Biddle was "but a boy" and his very appearance bespoke his innocence. The lawyer went on to note Biddle came from a "good family" and was not a trouble maker. He remarked the people who had identified Biddle on the night of the riot had testified the youth was wearing a round top hat, when, in fact, he had been wearing a slouch hat. He also noted the youth's testimony about being hurt by the mob was accurate as the rioters had "injured" many innocent people as they rampaged through the streets of Danville.

A. B. Dennis then took the floor and the young attorney, known as Bart by his friends, took a different tact than Chambers. He attacked the credibility of the prosecution witnesses. He noted the witnesses themselves had been at the scene of the violence on July 25th, yet they had not been indicted for rioting. He called S. F. Schecter a "would be " attorney and said the man had "lied" on the witness stand. He referred to Constable VanVickle as the "greatest falsifier" in the county of Vermilion and said the man was hiding behind a bedpost at the jail during the time of the attack.

At this point Judge Thompson asked the attorney to approach the bench and he warned the young man to "be careful" with his accusations. Dennis remarked he was only stating "facts." To this the judge firmly replied he was in a court of law and instructed him to conduct himself in a "professional manner."

Following the judge's reprimand, Dennis summed up his testimony. He stated there could be no doubt as to the defendants' innocence. He noted there was not one piece of evidence to show they had participated in the riot.

William Beckwith now took the floor. The crowd had been quiet during the fiery presentation by Dennis, now they became restive and Thompson had to quiet them down. The forty-five year old Beckwith was a seasoned attorney. His father, Hiram, had also been an attorney and had taken the law exam from Abraham Lincoln. Beckwith, like the other attorneys, pointed out there had been no evidence presented to show the defendants had committed any crime. He stated it was not the duty of the jurors to "punish" someone just because there had been a riot in Danville. It was "their duty " to decide the guilt or innocence of those before them "strictly" on the evidence presented.

The grandson of Danville's namesake, Dan Beckwith, noted while Jack Walton might "unquestionably be guilty of being drunk and disorderly," there was no evidence to show he was guilty of any other crimes. He further noted the men now being tried were no more guilty than were the hundreds of others who had gathered at the jail on the night of July 25th.

Charles Brown then took the stand and began to make an eloquent appeal on behalf of the defendants. Though the thirty-seven year old attorney had just been admitted to the bar the previous year, his efforts were that of a seasoned attorney. He noted most of the men were family men, they had young children who would suffer if they were convicted. Brown looked to the courtroom and pointed out it was filled with "family members" who were concerned for those now on trial. He walked to the row of defendants and pointed to them, "these men are not criminals," he said, his voice rising. "These are working men, no more guilty than you or me."

Brown then said there had been no evidence presented that could possibly convict the men. He further noted Noah Jones, one of the prosecution witnesses, was one of the most villainous men in the county; adding any testimony he had given should be "regarded as a pack of lies."

Keeslar jumped to his feet and objected to Brown's statement, but Brown raised his voice and continued his attack on Jones. Judge Thompson had to shout at the attorney, who had began with such an eloquent delivery, to quiet him down. Now he asked Brown to approach the bench.

He told the lawyer he must observe the "rules of decorum" in the courtroom. He further noted if Brown did not know or understand those rules, he would give him a few lessons. The subdued attorney finished his argument and returned to his seat. He made no further attack on the prosecution witnesses.

George Salmons then took his turn for the defense. The attorney walked to the jury box and began to speak in a low voice. His delivery was marked by pity, eloquence, and satire.

He said it was indeed unfortunate a few innocent people had been singled out of a crowd of thousands to be punished for crimes committed by others. These people, he pointed at the defendants, have already been shot, jailed, and now are being tried for crimes carried out by others.

It was clear to those watching that Salmons seemed to be reaching some jurors with his appeal. It was noticed the jurors nodded in agreement, and all seemed to be moved by the attorney's words.

Salmons walked over and stood beside Jack Walton and told the jurors to "look at the defendants." These "men and boys" are not criminals, he told them. "These are working members of the community."

He stated some of the men are fathers. "What purpose," Salmons questioned "will it serve to break up families?" "Take a good look at

Jack Walton," he said, resting a hand on Walton's shoulder. "There's not a finer person around than Jack."

Salmons noted on the night of the riot, "poor Jack was as full as a goose, and if he assaulted the jail, it must have been with the jawbone of an ass."

The attorney carefully went over each man's case, noting each had clearly proven he was innocent. He explained not one, but many, witnesses had come forward to testify to the men's lack of guilt.

Salmons closed by declaring to the jurors, the men on trial are no more guilty than "you and me." He pointed out it could just as easily have been one of "us," for the men arrested had been picked at random. There can only be one verdict, he told the eleven jurors who were listening intently, and that is "innocent for all the accused."

It had taken the defense a little less than two and a half hours to make its statements. Now State's Attorney Keeslar stood and walked to face the jury. He was quiet a few seconds and then he turned and pointed at the defendants.

"These are fine specimens to try to override law and order in Vermilion County," he stated.

He noted young Bell had just been released from reform school two months previous and Adam Murray was an admitted "penitentiary bird."

He asked the jury if they thought a man of Whitlock's reputation and character would take his riot gun and shoot innocent people. He asked if the jury thought a man like Deputy Newlin, one of the finest citizens in the county, would take his revolver and shoot to kill a man who was doing absolutely nothing.

Keeslar said the defense witnesses had delivered inconclusive and conflicting testimony. He noted there was a question as to what the witnesses "themselves" were doing at the jail during the violence.

The prosecutor pointed out the mob had been warned repeatedly to leave the streets, but they had persisted in their lawless rampage. They had thrown rocks at the lawmen, shot at the Sheriff and the jail, and butchered and burned a human being on the streets of Danville.

Keeslar went over each case, carefully placing the defendant at the jail. He then said the defendants had been given every chance to disperse but they had ignored the warnings of Whitlock. As a last resort, the lawman had stopped them at the very door of the county jail with his shotgun. Those wounded had been in the act of trying to break into the jail. He stated Bell had only been a few feet, possibly a few inches, from the shotgun when he was felled. The small, thin attorney, closed by asking for a verdict of guilty as charged for all the defendants.

The case was given to the jury shortly before noon and once again the defendants were taken back to the jail. Those who had gathered in and around the courthouse dispersed for the noon hour. It was speculated the jury would only be out a short time.

By 1:30 in the afternoon the courtroom was again filled with people waiting on the return of a verdict. Some thought all the men would be found innocent; there were others who thought they would all be pronounced guilty. As the afternoon wore on, and no verdict was returned, the room began to empty. By 5:00 P.M. only Judge Thompson and six spectators remained in the room which had been packed. When the judge left for the dinner hour, the others followed. Word leaked out the jury was hopelessly deadlocked.

Thompson returned to his courtroom about 7:00 P.M to await the jury. He was soon joined by a number of other people, many of them family members of the accused. As the evening hours wore away, people began to believe the jury was deadlocked. At 11:00 P.M. the judge went home. If the jury reached a verdict, they would call for him.

Saturday, August 29th dawned on a city still awaiting a verdict in the trial. It had been five weeks to the day since the murders and rioting in the city on the Vermilion had gained Danville national press coverage.

Now, as an early morning breeze stirred the leaves on the big cottonwood tree that stood north of the jail, people began to arrive in the city to do their weekly shopping. In stores and shops all over Danville, the main topic of conversation was the trial.

In the jury room in the courthouse, the eleven men were actively trying to reach a verdict. The last ballot they had cast had been ten for conviction of all the accused and one for a not guilty verdict for all. Tempers wore thin as those wanting a guilty verdict tried to convince William Pate, the lone juror holding out for a verdict of innocent, to change his vote. Pate remained steadfast in his stand and it began to appear there would be no verdict.

Saturday was always the busiest day of the week in the city. By mid-morning a number of buggies were drawn up next to the courthouse and men could be seen gathered about the building. As the men talked in small groups, armed soldiers periodically walked a patrol around the structure. By noon, when no verdict had been returned, those gathered around the courthouse dispersed.

The jury room was beginning to heat up as the noon hour passed. William Pate grudgingly made a concession as the hands on the clock in the room marked midday. He would vote guilty for Jack Walton and Winfield Baker, but he held out for a verdict of innocent for all the others. Tempers were also heated in the room and jury foreman, John Randall, had to calm the men down a number of times.

Sheriff Whitlock spent the day at the jail with his family. Since the riot and his defense of the jail, he had been called a hero and a villain. He had received praise from the President of the United States and criticism from the leaders of the Republican Party, his party, in his own state. Strangers had sent him messages of encouragement and money, county residents had threatened his life and that of his family. When asked years later if he thought he had made the right decision on the night of the riot, the lawman would answer there was no decision to be made, he just did his duty.

Now, as the day wore away into evening, it looked as if there would be no verdict against the accused. Through the hours of the afternoon, the other jurors continued to try to convince Pate to change his decision, but he would not budge. He in turn asked the others to join him in his decision.

Darkness had long since fallen on the city when juror Hoffman, a farmer from Sidell, Illinois, told the others that he was a very devout man. He would not take any part in reaching a decision on the Sabbath. The clock on the wall showed the other jurors the Sabbath was less than two hours away. Hoffman further told them he would be in a "torpid" state on Sunday and would not even discuss the trial.

The thought of spending all day Sunday locked up in a room in the courthouse with no chance of reaching a decision did not set well with the other jurors, Pate included. The rest of the members went to work on him with an added fervor and soon reached a compromise. At 11:15 P.M. word was sent out that a verdict had been reached.

Judge Thompson was notified and the Sheriff was told to get his prisoners dressed and back to the courthouse. It took some time for all the parties to assemble and by the time they had all reached the courtroom it was midnight.

As the eight defendants stood to hear the verdict, the courtroom was almost empty. The only people present besides the jury, law court staff, and press were Laura Whitlock and Justice Grant. None of the defense lawyers were present for the reading of the verdict.

Jury Foreman John Randall handed the slip of paper to the court and the findings were read. Guilty for Winfield Baker, Jack Walton, Adam Murray, Isaac Slade, John Robertson, and Thomas Bell. Found not guilty were William Redwine and Clay Biddle. The only defendants to show any emotion at the verdict were Redwine and Biddle. Their relief was obvious as the not guilty verdict was read. As the defendants were marched away following the reading of the verdict, it was noted Winfield Baker's good humor seemed to have disappeared.

Even though Redwine and Biddle had been found innocent, they were locked up with the others for there were other charges against them still pending.

Chapter Twenty-two

August 30th saw the first trouble erupt between the defendants housed at the county jail. Winfield Baker and William Redwine had been cellmates since the men had been arrested. The two seemed to be good friends as they spent their weeks of captivity quietly in their cell playing cards. But following the verdict of Saturday night, they spent the predawn hours of Sunday morning heatedly arguing.

Baker had pointed out to anyone who would listen that Redwine and Biddle were as guilty as the rest of the defendants. Redwine had been heard gloating over the fact he had been found innocent. The disagreement finally reached the point where Baker told the other man he was going to turn "state's evidence" in the coming trial. The trial yet to take place would have the harshest penalties for those found guilty. On hearing this, Redwine stopped talking and started swinging.

Both men were strong, big men, but Baker was giving Redwine a good beating when the construction worker managed to get his teeth into the Kentuckian's finger. Redwine chewed with such vigor on the finger that Baker was frantically trying to save it when deputies arrived to break up the fight. A doctor had to be summoned to sew up Baker's injured finger. The two men were placed in separate cells for the duration of their stay at the county jail.

August 31st through September 3rd saw the court trying to assemble a jury for the final trial. The press referred to it as the big trial because it would have the most defendants and would carry the stiffest sentences. There was also speculation no jury would convict Bessie Dodge, the only woman arrested for taking part in the violence.

As the last day of August and the first day of September passed, over a hundred possible jurors were dismissed because they declared themselves "hopelessly prejudiced." When all the names had been drawn from the boxes, Thompson once again began sending out for potential jurors. He first called a number of businessmen whom he thought would make acceptable jurors.

As these individuals declared, one after the other, they had a strong opinion regarding the case, Thompson delivered some sharp messages on their responsibilities as citizens. He also hinted the real reason men did not want to serve was because they did not want to take time away from their work.

As the second day of the new month passed there were still not enough jurors to try the case. Bessie Dodge had become ill on the previous day and had been dismissed from the courtroom. She would not attend any of the pre-trial sessions. Winfield Baker and William Redwine sat at opposite ends of the row of defendants, both men's faces were bruised and Baker wore a bandage on his finger. The Kentuckian's normal good spirits had disappeared and he looked sullen as he watched the proceedings.

September 3rd saw Thompson at last fill the jury box. The number of prospective jurors that had passed through the courtroom far surpassed the previous number heard for any trial in the county's history. Judge Thompson had taken an active part in attempting to impanel a fair jury.

Thompson also would make some changes in the courtroom for the coming trial. He was going to curb some of the problems he had incurred during the previous two trials. The public had been all too free in expressing itself during the previous court proceedings. There had been cat calls, offers of advice, and complaints about the accommodations in the courtroom. These interruptions had taken place while court was in session, and Thompson had suffered them for nearly two weeks. Now, with fourteen defendants ready to be seated in the room and "half the attorneys" in Danville presiding, there would be some new rules. Only officers of the court, attorneys, and newsmen would be allowed to occupy the space behind the railing in the courtroom.

The fourteen to be tried in the final trial were Winfield Baker, Jack Walton, Adam Murray, Isaac Slade, William Redwine, John Robertson, Thomas Bell, Clements Mobaker, John Isom, Ol Manifield, Horace Murphy, Richard Roberts, John Kress, and Bessie

Dodge. The others who had been indicted would not come to trial, they would eventually plead guilty or have their cases dismissed.

The fourteen defendants were accused of assault with intent to commit murder. Among the fourteen were the ones who Whitlock and Keeslar considered to be the leaders of the mob. If found guilty, these people would go to prison.

With the stage set for the final chapter in the riot of 1903 to be written, the troops were at last withdrawn from the city of Danville. With some convictions already finalized, and the public seemingly willing to accept the jury's decision, the presence of soldiers was no longer considered a necessity.

Serving on the jury that would determine the fate of the last of the rioters to stand trial were: Oscar Baldwin, Danville; Fred Barrick, Elwood; Ed Foster, Middlefork; R. S. Jaggers, Sidell; Fred Grooms, Ross; D. H. Claypool, Newell; William Allison, Newell; Isaac Carter, Ross; J. E. Gilgris, Danville; Scott Hildrath, Danville; and H. L. Green, Oakwood.

September 4th was a Friday and it was the first day the defendants had been walked to the courthouse without troops nearby. Whitlock and four deputies guarded the fourteen handcuffed prisoners during the short walk to the place of the trial. The sidewalk was lined with spectators as the small group made their way. No one caused any trouble, and there were the usual good natured remarks aimed at Jack Walton. The prisoners moved at a slow pace, to accommodate the crippling injuries which Bell and some of the others had received during the riot.

Winfield Baker seemed to have regained his good humor that had disappeared after the fight with Redwine. There was speculation he might testify against the others, but one of the defendants would say later there was never a chance of that.

When the long line of prisoners filed into the courtroom, they found eight attorneys there ready to plead their cases. Bessie Dodge was pale and quiet as she took her seat at the end of the row of defendants. She wore a dark dress and a small hat was pinned to her red hair. The defiant attitude she had displayed during much of her confinement seemed to have fled.

State's Attorney Keeslar and attorney Salmons made the opening statements to the jury. Then the prosecutor called his first witness.

Noah Jones took the stand and testified against Redwine, as he had done in the previous trial. He was followed by Charles Lloyd who also testified against Redwine.

Then Keeslar called on Sheriff Whitlock. The big lawman was dressed in a dark suit and vest with a watch chain extending from his vest pocket.

The courtroom was quiet since Judge Thompson had made the changes in the seating arrangements. Whitlock looked at the line of defendants for a few seconds and then began his testimony.

His statements were the same as in the previous trials, but he gave additional testimony regarding the new defendants. He pointed Roberts out as the man who wanted to be part of a committee to search the jail for the Negro, Wilson. Whitlock noted Roberts had lost his hat during the riot.

The lawman pointed to Horace Murphy and said that individual was standing near the jail shouting, "Hang the nigger."

He pointed to Robertson and said he had told him to go home and the man had responded he would go home when "I damn well please."

He looked at Mobaker and testified he had seen him at the jail and the defendant had told him, "I don't give a damn about the niggers. Boots Monroe is the man I want to get." (Monroe was a white man in the jail accused of murder.) The lawman testified he had seen Isom in the jail yard, holding onto the rail, young Bell had been standing next to him. He recalled telling Bell to go home, that this was no place for boys.

He also warned Isaac Newton Slade he had better leave. Slade had replied, "There are too damned many niggers in the country and I'll go home when I get good and ready." Whitlock reported he saw Kress inside the jail yard. The lawman also identified Bessie Dodge as the woman who had stood in the back of a wagon shouting for the rioters to kill the Sheriff and "hang the niggers."

Whitlock was followed on the witness stand by deputies David Newlin, Charles Runyan, and Enoch Vanvickle. They gave the same testimony they had previously given. S. F. Schecter also testified as in the former trial.

William Armstrong, a resident of Washington Avenue, then took the stand. He testified he had been in the area of the jail shortly before midnight and he had seen a woman standing in front of the livery and feed barn across from the jail. He said the woman pointed to the smoldering body of John Metcalf and told a crowd of men who were gathered around her, "If you boys had any grit, you'd put the Sheriff where the nigger is." She also said, "It's a shame that two white men should be killed for a nigger."

Armstrong was the last witness to be called in the morning session and as the courtroom emptied for the noon recess, it was noted by the newsmen the trial was not going well for the defendants. Whitlock had delivered his strongest testimony of the trials and several new witnesses had been unshaken by the defense attorney's cross examinations.

Doctor Guy was the first prosecution witness called when the trial resumed in the afternoon. He testified he had treated a leg wound for Mince Mobaker on the night of the riot. Mobaker had been wounded by buckshot entering the back of his leg above the knee. The physician noted he had removed twenty-three to twenty-five shot from the eight inch wound. He once again testified he had treated Adam Murray and Thomas Bell. He estimated Bell had about seventy-five buckshot in his right thigh and right hand, adding that the youth was severely injured. Guy said he had also treated the wounds of several others, but they were not among the defendants. The physician's testimony confirmed the fact there were numerous people wounded on the night of violence who were not arrested.

Doctors Winslow and Fletcher also took the stand and each testified they had treated the wounded. Both had worked on Isaac Newton Slade when it was necessary to amputate one of his fingers.

George Jarvis testified he had seen Winfield Baker at the livery barn across from the jail at 11:00 P.M. The Kentuckian had come in for a drink of water. The livery man said Baker had a revolver in each hand when he came in. Attorney Salmons spent several minutes in his cross-examination of Jarvis, who had not appeared in the previous trials. The defense attorney asked if Jarvis did not first tell he saw the defendant come into the barn with a bundle in each hand and go and place them in his buggy. Jarvis denied he had told such a story and added he could not remember who he had first told his story to.

Jack Benning then took the stand and said he had observed a woman upon a wagon during the riot. He testified he had been to the jail twice during the evening and both times the woman was in the wagon, shouting for the mob to attack the jail. On cross-examination, Benning could not positively identify Bessie Dodge.

James P. Green, proprietor of Danville Transfer Co., next took the stand. Green lived on Pine Street, just a few blocks from the county jail. He said on the night of the violence three wounded men were brought to his barn. He said one of the men had his finger shot off and sat in a chair. The other two were more seriously wounded and they were laid out on the floor until an ambulance took them away. Green said he did not believe any of the three were among the defendants.

Henry Hunt, Fred Jahnke, and Mrs. Hunt followed Green, giving the same testimony they had given in the previous trial. When they had completed their appearance, it was growing late in the afternoon. Judge Thompson looked at the large clock ticking off the minutes in the courtroom and then adjourned the trial for the supper hour, informing the participants there would be a night session of court beginning at 6:30 P.M.

When the trial resumed, Joe Campbell of Hungry Hollow took the stand and testified against John Isom. He said the defendant came to his house on Sunday morning and told him he had a "hot time" in Danville Saturday night and he had been shot. He then displayed the wounds in his foot and ankle. On cross-examination Campbell admitted Isom had not said where he was when he was shot or what he had been doing.

John Thomas, a miner from Himrod, then took the stand. Thomas, also a prisoner at the county jail, testified against Murphy. He reported that in a jail house conversation, Murphy had told him he was shot at the jail. Salmons cross-examined Thomas and the witness became mixed up under the questioning, first admitting and then denying the same query. When the defense attorney was finished, it was noted by those watching that the testimony of Thomas was "questionable."

The town marshal of Rossville took the stand and testified against Ol Manifield. Marshal Evans testified he had arrested the farmhand on Monday, following the riot of the previous Saturday night. The lawman noted Manifield was still "pretty drunk" and he was boasting about the "big fight" he had "with niggers" in Danville on Saturday night. He told the lawman "you ought to have been there." The officer said he placed the farm worker in the "calaboose." The next day, when Manifield had sobered up, he denied the story of the previous day.

Evans was the last witness for the prosecution and Thompson allowed the defense to call only one witness as the hour was growing late. Winfield Baker took the stand and told the same story he had related in the previous trials. Keeslar briefly cross-examined the defendant and then took his seat. There was nothing new in the testimony or the examination by the state's attorney.

The hour was now nearing 10:00 P.M. and Judge Thompson adjourned the trial until the next morning. The long line of defendants was led from the courtroom, followed by their attorneys. Keeslar appeared to be tired after the long day in court as he walked out of the room with Sheriff Whitlock.

Chapter Twenty-three

Saturday, September 5th was a cool day in Danville. As the prisoners were led to the courthouse, many of their family members were among the line of people who watched them march along. Since Judge Thompson had limited the number of people in the courtroom, it was not possible for them to be near the accused in the trial room. It was a "bit pitiful" a news reporter noted, to hear the young children call out to their handcuffed fathers, being led along like a "bunch of sheep to the slaughter."

During the Saturday session of court it looked like there would be no surprises. As each defendant took the stand, they denied all the charges brought against them. They either denied being at the jail or said they were there only out of curiosity, as had been thousands of others on the night of the riot. Keeslar carefully cross-examined each person taking the stand but nothing new was accomplished by his questioning.

When Bessie Dodge made her appearance, the woman was so pale and nervous there was general speculation no jury would convict her. Gone was all the brashness and toughness she had exhibited previously. She testified in a quiet voice and when attorney Salmons was finished with questioning her, Keeslar made no move to cross-examine the witness.

Richard Roberts was called to the stand following Dodge. Attorney Salmons waited patiently as his witness walked slowly to the witness chair. The young defendant, who worked as a clerk at a West Main Street restaurant in Danville, was well composed as he took the oath.

Roberts testified he went to the jail during the trouble, drawn by the sound of the mob. He stated he took no part in the riot and he was only in front of the embattled building for about half an hour. He denied he had asked the Sheriff to put him on a committee to search the jail for the Negro, Wilson. When Salmons finished his examination and Keeslar walked forward to cross-examine, the most sensational testimony of the trial was about to be given.

When Keeslar asked, during his cross-examination, if Roberts had seen anyone he knew at the riot, the witness was quiet for a few seconds. Then he looked at the row of defendants and said "yes." He pointed at Jack Walton and said he had seen him in front of the jail yelling curses at Whitlock. He nodded at Winfield Baker and said he saw the Kentuckian throwing stones at the jail and breaking out the streetlights. He testified he had observed Adam Murray rallying the mob and shooting at the jail.

There had been an undercurrent of noise in the courtroom before Keeslar began his cross-examination. The people watching the trial had become accustomed to witness after witness telling the same story and their interest had began to wane. Now, as Roberts delivered his damning testimony, there was complete silence among those watching. The prisoners regarded their fellow defendant with hard stares, a hint of a smile played at the corners of Baker's mouth. The defense attorneys entered a number of objections but they were all overruled.

When Roberts pointed at Bessie Dodge, tears glinted in the woman's eyes. The witness said he saw the red haired Dodge urging on the mob and he heard her shout, "The Sheriff is no better than the niggers and he ought to be lynched, too." The clerk finished his testimony by telling Keeslar he had observed all the accused at the jail taking part in the violence.

When the prosecutor said he was done with the witness, Roberts slowly walked back to his chair in the row of defendants. Attorney Salmons frowned at Roberts and shook his head as the man sat down. Judge Thompson had to call for quiet as the people in the courtroom began to discuss the testimony they had just heard.

The rest of the trial was anti-climatic following the testimony of Roberts. The last witness was heard shortly before noon and the afternoon was to be taken up by the final arguments of the attorneys. As the courtroom emptied for the noon hour, it was generally agreed the testimony of Roberts had probably "did in" all the defendants.

When court reconvened, the defense attorneys and Keeslar were ready to deliver their closing arguments. It would be a repetition of what had already been heard. The defendants were already proclaiming they had been sold out by Roberts. There was speculation among their attorneys the restaurant worker had made a deal with Keeslar. As Roberts sat among his fellow defendants, it was clear he was very uncomfortable.

As the afternoon wore away, defense attorney after defense attorney made an earnest appeal for their client. Each of the eight men who had been representing the accused took his turn at pleading for them. But to the spectators in the courtroom, there did not seem to be the response to the pleas that had been exhibited in the first trial. No heads nodded in agreement and one reporter noted the "verdict" already seemed to be in as the attorneys continued their summation.

The defense attorneys were careful to stress the fact that because some of the defendants had been wounded, the wounds should not be considered proof of guilt. They pointed out the majority of the wounded had not been arrested.

Only when the case of Bessie Dodge was mentioned did the jurors seem in the least moved. As the woman sat in the long line of other defendants, occasionally wiping tears from her eyes, she drew sympathetic glances from the men on the jury.

Salmons again gave a strong performance as he once again told the jury it would serve "no purpose" to imprison these "working members" of the community. He repeated his earlier argument that their families would suffer. He pointed out the bullet scarred head of Adam Murray, the crippled hand with the missing finger which rested on the chair arm of Isaac Slade, and asked the jury, "haven't these men suffered enough?" But even as the strong voice of Salmons filled the high-ceilinged courtroom, the reporters were betting all but Bessie Dodge would be found guilty.

When the defense had finished, Keeslar slowly walked to the front of the room. Once again he went over each case, explaining why each should be found guilty. As he stood in front of the jury, the slender state's attorney pointed at the defendants. "It is true," he noted "that some of these men are family men, but," he added, "they have broken the law and had it not been for Sheriff Whitlock they would surely have committed murder." Keeslar pointed out the accused had now been "identified" by one of their own number as having "committed" the crimes they were indicted for. Roberts shifted nervously in his seat as the other defendants turned to look at him. Keeslar reminded the jurors that Sheriff Whitlock and his deputies had risked their lives to uphold the law. It was now time for the jurors to do their duty. He concluded the state had proven, far beyond any doubt, the rioters were guilty as charged. He then asked the jury to return a guilty verdict "for all" the accused.

It was 6:00 P.M. in the evening when Judge Thompson gave the jurors their instructions. They then retired to the jury room to discuss a verdict.

The long line of defendants were once more led down the sidewalk to the county jail. The sounds of Saturday night in Danville were beginning to fill the night as the procession filed slowly along, hampered by the crippled leg of Bell and the maimed knee of Mobaker. The tinny music of a piano floated out the open door of Shaffer's Saloon, just north of the jail. Streetcar bells clanged and the rhythmic sound of horses' hooves striking the brick streets echoed in the evening air.

Friends and relatives called out to the prisoners as they made their way to the jail, but the group was unusually silent as they walked along. When they reached the building, Sheriff Whitlock instructed his deputies to place Roberts in a cell separate from the other defendants. He did not want another jailhouse fight.

It was assumed by those involved in the trial and by the public no verdict would be reached before Monday since it was late in the day on Saturday. Judge Thompson went to his home on Pine Street and the other participants also left the courthouse. Some of the press people waited around until supper was served to the jurors, hoping to glean some information from the men who served the meals. When they were unable to wring any comment from the deputies, they too left the building.

In the jury room the jurors spent less time than had been expected deciding the case. The only defendant there was any large degree of disagreement over was Bessie Dodge. On the first ballot, a majority voted Dodge innocent. The vote was unanimous for the guilt of ten of the others and the innocence of two. Before the clock struck midnight a decision had been reached on Dodge and the bailiff at the door was notified.

Word was sent to Judge Thompson and the prisoners were routed out of the jail for a return trip to the courthouse. State's Attorney John Keeslar and defense attorney William Beckwith were on hand to hear the verdict.

As the accused filed into the courtroom and lined up before the judge, they appeared to be in a somber mood. Even the alleged leader of the group, Winfield Baker, had lost his happy go lucky attitude and was now quiet and withdrawn.

Jury Foreman Oscar Baldwin handed over the verdict and it was given to the grim faced Thompson in the dimly lit room. The defendants stood quietly in the nearly empty courtroom as the verdict was read; guilty for Jack Walton, William Redwine, Mince Mobaker, John Isom, Winfield Baker, John Robertson, Isaac Slade, Thomas Bell, Horace Murphy, Adam Murray, Ol Manifield, and Bessie Dodge. Not guilty for Richard Roberts and John Kress.

It was clear William Beckwith was not satisfied with the verdict rendered by the jury. He stood with the defendants during the reading of the verdict but he conversed with no one. When Judge Thompson asked the attorney if he wanted the jury polled, Beckwith only stared at the judge.

The press noted it was no surprise John Kress was found innocent. Kress was employed by the different saloon keepers about town to scrub out their establishments and was a "harmless soul" in the eyes of one reporter. In 1901 he had been afflicted with one of the "worst cases" of small pox in the "cities history" and it had left him badly "crippled."

It was thought Richard Roberts' testimony against the others had "bought" his verdict of innocence. Though Winfield Baker had not testified against the others, he had mentioned on more than one occasion "we are all guilty."

Judge Thompson thanked the jury for their services and discharged the men. The prisoners were sent back to the county jail.

As the guilty made their fourth trip over the same route on Saturday, September 5, 1903, the streets were nearly deserted. Only the saloons were doing a lively business in the sleeping city. Their footfalls echoed hollowly in the stillness of the night as they approached the jail. It had been five weeks ago, almost to the hour, when Whitlock had made his historic stand at this very spot. Now as the convicted rioters walked onto the porch of the jail, there were no crowds of supporters thronging the street. Years later Isaac Slade would remember, there were "men in every saloon in Danville, as guilty as we were, but no one identified them."

Eight others who had been indicted for the violence would not come to trial, they would plea bargain and serve time in the county jail or have their charges dismissed. The state's attorney had tried the individuals he had felt most responsible for the crimes committed on that historic Saturday.

Chapter Twenty-four

Following the trial, public interest in the riot and its aftermath began to fade. Vermilion County was returning to normal and Danville was no longer patrolled by armed soldiers. Even the "foreign" newspaper reporters had left the city.

A tax ferret hired by the county had just reported there were numerous residents who were not paying their property taxes and hadn't been for years. It was noted many of those on the "tax dodger" roll were prominent citizens of the county. The tax story immediately replaced the riot as the topic of conversation in the general stores and other public gathering places.

In the county jail, the convicted rioters were serving time as they awaited sentencing for their crimes. There would be one more appeal, but they held out little hope it would be successful. Sheriff Whitlock commented he was satisfied with the findings of the jury and he thought justice had been served. Whitlock privately noted he believed the individuals who had attempted to storm his jail were the same ones who had successfully assaulted the city building and murdered Metcalf, but he had no proof. The lawman was also acutely aware things would never be the same between he and many residents of the county.

On September 8th the Sheriff and his deputies escorted the twelve convicted rioters to the courthouse for the final time. There was a hint of autumn in the air as the handcuffed prisoners filed along Vermilion Street on their way to their last court appearance. A large crowd was gathered about the building to witness the last chapter in the legal proceedings of the riot of 1903. The Danville tragedy which had filled thousands of pages with newsprint across the state and the nation was about over.

When the ten men, one woman, and teenage boy had been seated in the defendants' chairs in Thompson's courtroom, the judge entered the room. There had been no restrictions placed on seating for this appeal sentencing session, so the judge was faced with a room filled to overflowing. The children and wives of the convicted were seated in the front while other relatives, friends, and the curious sat and stood in the back. A reporter noted it was a moving experience to witness the anguished looks on the faces of the wives and the tear filled eyes of the children as they watched their handcuffed husbands and fathers.

The defense attorneys had been vocal in their criticism of the way the trial had been conducted and now their appeal would echo with anger and frustration.

Defense Attorney Brown began the two hour appeal. He argued several rulings by the court had damaged the defense and had been unfair. He pointed out the defense had not been allowed to introduce key evidence. He reflected William Redwine told people he had been involved in the riot as a joke, but the prosecution had used the statement made in jest against the man. He stated attorney John Webster had violated the rules of the profession in regard to client-council relationship by testifying against the rioters. He argued the verdict certainly was not supported by evidence and the prosecution had failed to show the accused had intended to commit murder. He also raised the question of the whereabouts of the Negro, Jim Wilson. He noted the Sheriff had told the rioters Jim Wilson was not in the jail at the time of the riot. Brown questioned how people could be convicted of storming a building to kill a man when the object of their intent was not present in the building. He finished his appeal by noting there had been thousands of people rampaging on the streets of Danville on the night of July 25th. He argued it was wrong to single out a "few innocent people" to bear the punishment for the many.

Attorney Salmons followed Brown and the seasoned defense lawyer delivered a stirring appeal for a new trial. Salmons was an attorney with more than a quarter of a century of experience and the seasoning was evident in his delivery.

He argued the jury had been unfair in its decision, and seemed to have appointed themselves as a court of equity, rewarding Roberts for his testimony and paying no attention to his guilt or innocence.

He noted the state had made a much stronger case against Roberts than it had against several of the other defendants. Salmons pointed at Sheriff Whitlock and told the court "no less a man" than the Sheriff had identified Roberts as one of those who had wanted to search the jail for Wilson. Whitlock remained expressionless as many in the courtroom turned to look at him as Salmons kept his finger pointed at the lawman.

Salmons continued, walking slowly in front of the bench, his hands folded behind him. He said the jury had failed to give the accused the benefit of a reasonable doubt, they had instead extended that benefit to the state. He also argued the defense had been hampered throughout the trial with unfair rulings by the court which had damaged their cause. He then went through the cases, one by one, and made several points in each he felt should qualify the rioters for a new trial. The families and friends of the convicted watched the proceedings in silence, the clock on the courtroom wall could be heard ticking off the seconds during Salmons brief pauses.

The attorney now walked to face Judge Thompson directly, only a few feet separated the man with the power from the one making the appeal. Salmons told the judge he must know the trial had been a mockery of justice. Thompson regarded the lawyer with a slight smile, like a teacher regarding a wayward student with patience and a touch of humor. Salmons then asked him "in the name of fairness" to grant all the defendants a new trial.

As Salmons took his seat, attorney Dennis slowly stood up. The youthful lawyer smiled at Bessie Dodge as he walked to the front of the room. The red-haired Dodge did not return the smile, but continued to rub one hand with the other, looking sad and frightened.

Dennis pointed out there had never been a woman convicted of inciting a riot in Vermilion County previous to the conviction of Dodge. He argued her conviction was a great "miscarriage of justice" and should be erased from the record. He asked the judge to observe the poor creature, noting she was a casualty of a legal system "bent on revenge." Dennis argued any remarks Dodge might have made were "made after the attack on the jail had taken place." He noted she could hardly be considered guilty of inciting a riot if it had already taken place before she said anything. If ever there was just cause for a new trial Dennis proclaimed, "this is certainly the time." He then walked to his seat.

The last attorney to speak was William Beckwith. When the others had finished, there was a brief pause in the proceedings as attorney Beckwith studied his notes. Then he stood and walked to the front of the room, looking briefly at the picture of Lincoln hanging prominently on the wall. He began to speak. It is not a question as to whether the convicted deserve a new trial or not he noted, the question is "will they get the trial they deserve?" Judge Thompson seemed to be studying his clasped hands as Beckwith spoke.

Beckwith then made an appeal on behalf of Jack Walton. "Look at Jack," he said, "does this man look like a criminal?" Walton smiled at the attorney, looking slightly self-conscious as heads turned in his direction. The attorney stated on the night of the riot, Walton was so drunk he did not know where he was or what he was doing and all he did was talk. He said it was impossible for a man in Walton's condition to be intent on anything, criminal or otherwise. There were a few smiles in the courtroom as Beckwith continued his appeal, noting Walton was a hard working family man and an asset to the community. The attorney pointed out the jury had failed to look at the evidence, which he felt was not substantial. Beckwith then approached the judge and asked a new trial be granted so "a wrong can be righted."

Beckwith was finished, and as he walked slowly toward his chair, all eyes turned to Judge Thompson. The courtroom became silent as people waited for Thompson to speak. The sounds of the outside world penetrated the silence as the bell of a streetcar clanged and a pigeon fluttered at a courtroom window.

Thompson took a few moments to regard the prisoners and the people packed into his courtroom before he spoke. He studied the apprehensive faces of the wives and families of the convicted men and the tear stained face of Bessie Dodge. He looked at the expressionless faces of State's Attorney Keeslar and Sheriff Hardy Whitlock as the two men sat silently watching the proceedings.

The judge then announced his decision, it was as expected and it was dreaded by the convicted. He overruled all motions for a new trial. He went over the past trial, pointing out he could find no fault with the verdict, remarking if he had been on the jury he would have made the same decision.

Thompson then addressed the prisoners, he knew some of the men personally. He noted it was a sad thing and a hard ordeal for their families, but they had no one to blame but themselves. He referred to those he knew and ended up speaking of Jack Walton.

"I have known Jack Walton for fifteen years," Thompson declared, his voice filling the quiet room. "No man in Danville is a better man sober than Jack Walton sober, and no man in Danville is a meaner man drunk than Jack Walton drunk. He has a good heart but whiskey turns it upside down. Jack Walton sober and Jack Walton drunk - it is another case of Dr. Jekyll and Mr. Hyde."

The judge told the prisoners they should thank God they were not being sentenced for murder instead of attempted murder and they weren't being sentenced to hang instead of the penitentiary. His voice rose and he looked intently at the convicted lined up before him. "For, as sure as you live, had you gained entrance to the jail that night, you would have committed murder, not once, but probably a dozen times. And if the right man had not been sheriff, you would have succeeded."

The courtroom remained quiet as the judge, who had grown to manhood on the prairie of central Illinois, began his sentencing. The first to be named was Bessie Dodge, the woman who had urged the mob on as they sought to break into the jail. Thompson sentenced her to an indeterminate sentence at the prison for women in Joliet. Next was young Thomas Bell, whose wounds from Whitlock's shotgun blast were still healing. Bell, who was a minor, was sent back to the reformatory at Pontiac, where he had been before coming to Danville.

The judge then read off the names of the ten convicted men and sentenced each of them to an indeterminate period of time to be served at the state penitentiary at Chester. As the sentences were announced, some of the women and children began to sob openly. Relatives began to move toward the front of the room but were stopped by the deputies who stood near the prisoners. The final curtain was being drawn on the riot of 1903.

Thompson pounded his gavel and the noise in the room subsided as the people who were moving became still. He commended Sheriff Hardy Whitlock for doing what no other lawman had ever done in handling the rioters. He praised the deputies and others who had stood by the Sheriff through a trying period. Lastly he noted prosecutor Keeslar had taken the "high road" in seeing the law of the land was carried out to "the end." Thompson then instructed Whitlock to take charge of his prisoners and the last court session for the Danville rioters was concluded.

Whitlock had maintained a rigid attitude with his prisoners during the trial and their time in jail. He now instructed his deputies to allow them as long as they needed to say their good-byes to families. Bessie Dodge and Winfield Baker moved to the side as wives, children, and other relatives surrounded the other prisoners. Dodge and Baker did not have anyone in the room, but Laura Whitlock walked forward and said a few words to the red-haired Dodge. Baker smiled and joked with newsmen as he waited to be taken back to the jail.

After several minutes had passed the convicted were lined up and moved from the courthouse back to the jail, many family members walking beside them. A reporter noted it would have been a "hard heart, indeed, that would not have been moved by all the tears shed by the wives and children of the convicted men."

Chapter Twenty-five

At 4:00 A.M. on September 9th, Whitlock and three of his deputies moved the ten convicted men to the C. & E.I. depot in Danville. In the predawn coolness of the September morning, they boarded a passenger train for the prison at Chester, Illinois.

While the Sheriff and his men were delivering the prisoners to the state penitentiary, the Vermilion County Board was considering the expenses created by the riot. There were men on the board who were not accustomed to a legal system that worked, where influence and bribery were ineffective. Now they had a chance to at least cause Whitlock a few problems for the way he had handled the riot case. Among the bills to be considered was one for $620 from Whitlock for pay for extra deputies and overtime costs, a direct result of the riot.

A number of the board members at once called the bill exorbitant and moved it not be paid. They stated Whitlock had spent the money "without approval," now let him "find the money" in his budget. Others pointed out there was not sufficient money to be "found" in Whitlock's budget. A long debate followed with heated exchanges from board members on both sides of the issue.

It was finally Supervisor Fisk who spoke out strongly for paying the bill. He noted Whitlock had saved the county jail from being destroyed by the mob. He declared Whitlock had accomplished "what no other sheriff had ever done." He had stopped a mob at his jailhouse door and saved the lives of a number of prisoners. Fisk noted Whitlock had risked not only his own life, but his family, in seeing the law of the land was carried out. He asked the board where "was everyone else" when a mob was butchering and burning a human being on the main streets of Danville? He observed Whitlock should be rewarded for his courage instead of being penalized by a backward board that sought revenge on a man of principle. Supervisor Canaday joined Fisk and pushed for the bill to be paid. The board then voted that the bill be paid but instructed $2.73 be deducted to pay back taxes owed by Deputy Hall.

Supervisor J. M. Carter offered a resolution thanking Sheriff Whitlock, his deputies, Judge Thompson, and the juries for the part they had played in seeing justice done. The resolution was adopted by the county board.

On September 14th, Sheriff Whitlock and his wife escorted Bessie Dodge to the women's prison in Joliet, Illinois. She was the last prisoner to be delivered, as young Tom Bell had previously been taken to the reformatory at Pontiac. Dodge had reportedly lost all of her toughness during her time in jail and was described as a "pitiful, scared woman" when she made the trip with the Whitlocks to Joliet.

Finis

Because of his actions during the hot summer of 1903, Hardy Whitlock became a role model for law enforcement agencies all over the nation. He was called upon to deliver numerous speeches. He wrote a letter putting down his procedures for handling riot situations, and copies were mailed to all the sheriffs in the state of Illinois, as well as to lawmen in many other states. Following Whitlock's example, other law enforcement people took a more determined stand against those who would take prisoners from their custody.

Hardy Whitlock never sought higher office, but he did become county treasurer, following his term as sheriff. As county teasurer he instituted many reforms and balanced the county budget. He lived out a full life, spending his later years in Detroit, Michigan. He passed away in 1948 at the age of 81, and was buried in his native Georgetown, Illinois, next to his wife Laura. During his long life, the man worked at many different things, but it was those terrible hours on a dark night in Danville, Illinois, when his courage and belief in the law gained him a place in history.

One of the treasures of the old lawman was found among his effects after he died. It was a telegram, yellowed with age. He had received the missive following his defense of the jail in 1903. It carried the same message as had hundreds of other telegrams he had received following his heroic stand. It lauded him for doing his duty. It was the signature that stood out; it was signed President Theodore Roosevelt.

There were no more lynchings in Vermilion County, Illinois.

INDEX